Bazaar
Property Doctor

D0540313

Bazaar
Property Doctor

Ian Morris
FRICS, MIAS, ACIArb

BBC Books

Acknowledgements

I would like to thank my professional colleagues who helped with checking the technical content of this book, in particular Peter Eaton, Malcolm Hollis, Peter Maton and John Perkins.

The illustrations on pages 59 and 60 are reproduced by permission of the Consumers Association.

I am also grateful to Jenny for typing the manuscript, to Suzanne for being so patient, and to Sandy for being so tolerant.

Published by BBC Books
A division of BBC Enterprises Ltd
Woodlands, 80 Wood Lane, London W12 0TT

First published 1989
© Ian Morris 1989
ISBN 0 563 21409 0

Typeset in 10/11 pt Helvetica
by Ace Filmsetting Ltd., Frome, Somerset
Printed and bound in Great Britain
by Richard Clay Ltd., Bungay, Suffolk
Cover printed by Fletchers of Norwich

Contents

Introduction

Most of us wish to keep in good health and to enjoy a long life. We want to avoid maladies of any kind – anyone not sharing this view would be regarded as abnormal.

When we are unwell few of us are expert enough to diagnose the problem and prescribe the right cure, but we try to familiarise ourselves with unhealthy symptoms so that, if nothing else, we know when it is necessary to consult a doctor.

So it should be with the buildings we live in. Our homes are valuable commodities, yet none last for ever. The materials of which every house is built deteriorate every day from the date of construction, and eventually wear out altogether. Whether or not we are expert enough to do our own repairs, we should know what to look out for. It should then be possible to deal with a problem straight-away, or get specialist advice if necessary, before a serious situation arises.

Some kinds of building repairs are expensive; many are *very* expensive, and even the smallest of repairs can become more expensive if ignored. The old saying 'a stitch in time saves nine' holds true for most building repairs.

In each section of this book you will find a heading entitled 'What to look out for', to help you to diagnose problems which could arise. A basic knowledge of the building you live in is helpful in planning routine main-tenance, so most sections of the book also include a heading called 'Get to know . . .'.

This book is not intended to be a DIY manual. It is more like the handbook you get when you buy a car: a guide to help you if problems arise, to show you how your home 'works', and to help you keep it in good working order.

The most common features of domestic building con-struction are included but, because of the wide range of building materials and the variation in building methods used throughout the country, and over the years, it is possible that some features of your own home may not be covered by this book.

Outside your House

Roofs

Your roof is obviously a vital part of your home, especially as it has to contend with the British climate. It is essential to make sure there is no risk of water penetration through the roof, otherwise the rest of the structure will be at risk.

Get to know your roof

Unless you are a keen do-it-yourselfer you are unlikely ever to see your roof at close hand. It will be helpful, therefore, and may even save you money in builders' time, if you can describe your roof accurately when calling on professional assistance.

Roofs are either pitched or flat, or sometimes a combination of the two. A mansard roof has two different pitches on the same side, the lower one being steeper; a hipped roof has all sides sloping inwards and upwards; other designs of pitched roofs may include gable ends or valleys (*see Figure 1*). The most useful thing to know about a pitched roof is what it is covered with – and you can normally discover this from a ground-level inspection, or by looking out of an upstairs window.

Modern pitched roofs are mostly covered with con-

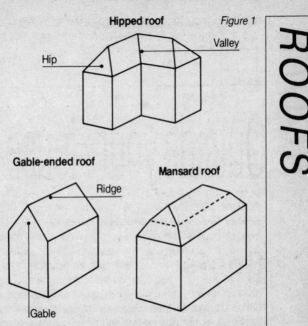

Hipped roof   *Figure 1*

Valley

Hip

Gable-ended roof

Ridge

Mansard roof

Gable

ROOFS

crete tiles; older roofs with slates, clay tiles, stone tiles, wooden shingles or thatch. Other materials used for pitched roofs include roofing felt and asbestos-cement sheets or slates (or asbestos-free cement slates in recent years). Metal coverings, such as lead, zinc and copper, are rarely found on pitched roofs of domestic buildings. They are, however, used around dormers (projecting structures, usually provided for building vertical windows into sloping roofs) and for forming weathertight joints – for example, at the intersection of two roof pitches, or as a flashing (at the junction between a roof covering and an adjoining wall).

Cement mortar fillets are sometimes found at the junction between a slate or tile roof and an adjoining wall or chimney; these fillets tend to crack and are seldom as reliable as a properly formed metal flashing.

If it looks as though your roof is sagging, the structure

9

ROOFS

Typical lifespan of roofing materials   *Figure 2*

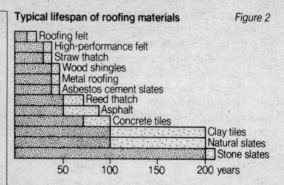

itself may be at fault. Many old structures were not built to today's standards and excessive deflection in the timbers can occur with age. The problem can easily arise if an old roof covering is renewed with heavier materials (slates replaced with concrete tiles, for example) and in such an instance you should always have the structure itself checked. It may well be possible to build in additional timbers to strengthen an otherwise weak roof structure, but advice on this should be obtained from a properly qualified professional, to ensure that alterations to the structure do not transfer weight incorrectly.

Whereas pitched roofs are almost always built with a timber framework, flat roofs can be of solid (concrete) or timber-framed construction. (The timber-built type is much more common in domestic buildings.) Asphalt is normally used for the weatherproof covering on a solid flat roof, while roofing felt is used on a timber-built structure. Modern high-performance membranes look similar to roofing felt, but are made almost entirely of synthetic materials and have a much greater life expectancy. Older flat roofs of timber construction may be covered with zinc or lead sheets.

Flat roofs are not intended to be completely flat, but should have a gradient of at least 1 in 40. Problems can arise where flat roofs have inadequate gradients. Unfortunately, it is usually a complicated and expensive job to improve the gradient of an existing flat roof.

If leaks occur in a flat roof, you should check the condition of the deck, to which the roof covering is fixed, before simply repairing or renewing the roof covering. Wood chipboard, and certain other types of panels used for roof decks, can be permanently damaged once saturated.

All roofs which contain insulation should be adequately ventilated – something which is frequently overlooked when insulation is installed in a previously unventilated roof. Unventilated roofs can attract condensation, and this can have a harmful effect on the timbers.

ROOFS

WHAT TO LOOK OUT FOR

SLATES AND TILES

▶ **Symptom**
Water penetration, with no obvious signs of damaged slates or tiles.

▶ **Cause**
a Wind blowing rain under the slates or tiles (and no underfelt).
b Defective flashings.
c Inadequate gradient to the roof slope(s), caused by poor design, or slates or tiles which are unsuitable for a low 'pitch'.

▶ **Remedy**
a Consider sealing the underside of the slates or tiles (torching), or re-roof with underfelt.
b Check or repair flashings.
c Consider using a different kind of tile suitable for a low 'pitch'.

▶ **Symptom**
Slates or tiles are broken; water penetration is possible.

ROOFS

▶ Cause
a Excessive weathering.
b Damage from excessive pressure (e.g., by people walking on the roof covering).

▶ Remedy
Replace the damaged slates or tiles.

▶ Symptom
The surface of slates, or clay tiles, is flaking (laminating); water penetration is possible.

▶ Cause
a Excessive weathering, or poor quality of the original slates or tiles; water gets into the slates or tiles and substantial damage can result if freezing occurs.
b Old age.

▶ Remedy
Replace the affected slates or tiles – either individually or over the whole roof slope(s).

▶ Symptom
Slates or tiles are missing, or have slipped out of place; water penetration is possible.

▶ Cause
a Slates – the fixing nails are corroded.
b Tiles – the holding nibs have broken off the back of the tiles.
c Tiles – storm damage has dislodged the tiles.

▶ Remedy
a Slates – remove defective slates and fix replacements, using copper clips (known as tingles); consider re-roofing if the problem is acute.
b Tiles – replace or renew the affected tiles.

c Renew the timber fixing battens if necessary.

▶ **Symptom**
Ridge or hip tiles are displaced or missing.

▶ **Cause**
a Storm damage has dislodged the tiles.
b The mortar bedding is excessively weathered.

▶ **Remedy**
Re-bed the ridge or hip tiles in cement mortar.

WOODEN SHINGLES

▶ **Symptom**
Splits in the shingles.

▶ **Cause**
The fixing nails have become corroded; or excessive weathering.

▶ **Remedy**
Replace defective shingles using nails which have a protective coating.

THATCH

▶ **Symptom**
The thatch becomes brittle.

▶ **Cause**
Old age, or birds nesting in the thatch, which reduces its life.

▶ **Remedy**
Maintain the wire netting to prevent birds nesting. Check the condition of the ridge every five years.

ROOFS

ROOFS

This work is best carried out by an experienced thatcher.

CORRUGATED SHEETS

▶ **Symptom**
Cracks or holes in the sheets.

▶ **Cause**
Generally old age; asbestos–cement sheets are easily damaged by excessive weight applied to their surface, which softens with age.

▶ **Remedy**
It is rarely worth trying to repair corrugated iron or asbestos–cement sheets; replace entire sheets and renew the fixing bolts. Do not break asbestos–cement sheets and keep dust to a minimum.

LEAD AND ZINC SHEET

▶ **Symptom**
a Splits or holes in the surface.
b Wrinkles in lead sheets.

▶ **Cause**
a Generally old age. Moss growth and other acid solutions can cause corrosion. Certain types of fixing nails also cause corrosion.
b The lead sheets are inadequately secured, or there is insufficient allowance for thermal expansion.

▶ **Remedy**
a Small defects can be repaired with soldered dots, or patches of the same metal; complete sheets should be replaced if the problem is extensive or if the metal is old and brittle. Copper fixing nails should be used.
b Complete sheets may need to be replaced. It may

be possible to shorten sheets which have expanded, and to form new joints with adequate fixings.
Repairs should be left to an experienced builder or plumber.

ASPHALT

▶ **Symptom**
a Bubbling or cracking.
b Surface lifting.
c Upstands at the perimeter falling away.

▶ **Cause**
a Moisture trapped under the asphalt.
b Thermal expansion of the asphalt.
c Weight and/or age of the asphalt.

▶ **Remedy**
Cut out the affected area and renew with new asphalt.
This work should be carried out by a specialist asphalt contractor.

▶ **Symptom**
General deterioration of the surface.

▶ **Cause**
The surface has been affected by excessive weathering (i.e., old age).

▶ **Remedy**
Renew the roof covering.
This work should be carried out by a specialist asphalt contractor.

ROOFS

ROOFS

BITUMINOUS FELT

▶ **Symptom**
Blisters, bubbling on the surface, or the vertical upstands falling away.

▶ **Cause**
a Poor materials and/or workmanship or an inadequate gradient in the roof structure.
b Moisture under the roof covering.

▶ **Remedy**
Patch repair, or renew the entire roof covering if the problem is extensive. Consider the use of high-performance materials for re-roofing.

▶ **Symptom**
Cracks and tears in the roof surface.

▶ **Cause**
a Movement in the structure of the roof (e.g., drying out or thermal movement).
b The surface has been affected by excessive weathering (i.e., old age).

▶ **Remedy**
Patch repair, or renew the entire roof covering if the problem is extensive. Build in an allowance for movement of the roof structure, if necessary. Consider the use of high-performance materials for re-roofing.

▶ **Symptom**
Crazing of the roof surface.

▶ **Cause**
The surface has been affected by excessive weathering (i.e., old age).

▶ **Remedy**

Renew the entire roof covering. Cover it with stone chippings bedded in bitumen, for protection. Consider the use of high-performance materials for re-roofing.

VALLEYS AND FLASHINGS

▶ **Symptom**

The roof is leaking at a valley or flashing.

▶ **Cause**

a Defective materials or workmanship.
b Insufficient overlap between the roof covering and the slates or tiles.

▶ **Remedy**

a Repair or replace – see the section on Lead and Zinc Sheet, page 14.
b Extend the roof covering or valley, or improve the method of weatherproofing at the edges of the metal.

▶ **Symptom**

The roof is leaking at a flashing between the roof covering and adjoining brickwork.

▶ **Cause**

a Metal flashing is inadequately sealed to the brickwork.
b There are insufficient or inadequate soakers under the slates or tiles.

▶ **Remedy**

a Cut a groove in the wall or chimney 150 mm (6 in.) above the level of the roof covering, turn the metal flashing at least 25 mm (1 in.) into the groove, fix it in place with metal wedges and seal with cement mortar.

ROOFS

b Provide metal soakers at every course of slates or tiles (not necessary with interlocking tiles).

Chimneys

Get to know your chimneys

Do you know how many chimneys there are around your property? Do you know how many flues there are in each chimney, and do you know whether any of the flues have been capped off?

If you have an older house, it is worth checking to see whether any of the chimney stacks are in poor condition. Try to view each chimney from two sides, at right-angles to each other, in each case visually lining up the side of the chimney stack with a structure you believe to be vertical. If you think one of your chimneys is significantly out of plumb, then get a surveyor or a reliable builder to take a closer look.

If chimneys are cement-rendered, it is possible that cracks may have allowed water to get behind this and loosen the rendering; a close check will reveal whether or not the rendering is intact.

Disused or redundant flues should be capped off and ventilated. Broken or loose chimney pots should be renewed or secured, or removed altogether if the flue is redundant. Make sure your chimney pots are secure - you live underneath them.

WHAT TO LOOK OUT FOR

CHIMNEYS

▶ **Symptom**

Loose brickwork; unstable chimney stack; a chimney leaning to one side.

▶ **Cause**
a Excessive weathering of the brick joints.
b Excessive condensation inside the flue or chemical reaction within the mortar.

▶ **Remedy**
Rake out and repoint the brick joints with cement mortar. Replace defective bricks and/or cement rendering (if the brickwork is rendered). Take down and rebuild the chimney if necessary. Consider the installation of a flue lining.

▶ **Symptom**
A broken or unstable chimney pot.

▶ **Cause**
Excessive weathering or condensation at the head of the chimney stack; or old age.

▶ **Remedy**
a Replace or refix the chimney pot.
b Cap off the flue (but incorporate ventilation).

▶ **Symptom**
A roof leak around the chimney.

▶ **Cause**
Defective flashing or cement fillets.

▶ **Remedy**
a See the section on Valleys and Flashings, page 17.
b Repair the cement fillets or replace them with metal flashings.

CHIMNEYS

External Walls

It obviously goes without saying that the external walls are a most important part of your home. Frequently neglected, they are not only supposed to keep the weather out and the warmth in, but they also provide essential structural support for other parts of the building.

Get to know your walls

The possible combinations of materials and ways in which your walls might be built are enormous, but the following is a general guide:

The structure
   masonry (e.g., brick or stone);
   steel- or concrete-framed;
   timber-framed;
   – or a combination of these.

The outer finish (for weather resistance)
   the structure alone (e.g., brickwork or stonework);
   cement rendering (sometimes with a pebbledash finish);
   cladding (e.g., tiling, timber boarding, plastic boards, concrete panels, etc.).

The structure itself may be solid, or may incorporate a cavity. There is some controversy about when cavity walls were first invented, but few buildings were constructed in this way before 1900. The cavity provides a measure of thermal insulation in itself, and also provides a barrier against penetrating damp if the outside of the wall is porous in any way. Filling a cavity with an insulating material is normally not harmful to the structure, provided the outside of the wall is completely weathertight.

   Most cavity-built walls have two 'leaves' of masonry, separated by a space of about 50 mm (2 in.), the two leaves being held together with cavity ties (usually made of metal); the ties are spaced about 900 mm (36 in.) apart and built into the masonry every 450 mm (18 in.) in height. Traditionally, the outer leaf of a cavity-built wall is

EXTERNAL WALLS

of brickwork, whereas the inner leaf may be built with bricks, breeze blocks, or aerated concrete blocks for better thermal insulation.

Modern timber-framed buildings have cavity-built outside walls. The inner leaf of the construction is the timber frame, and this is the structural part of the wall, while the outer leaf (of brickwork, for example) is for weather resistance; again, metal ties are built in to hold the two leaves together.

Another kind of construction consists of a steel or concrete framework to which cladding is fixed externally and a lightweight wall is fixed internally.

How do you know if a brick wall is solid or cavity-built? Short of breaking it open and having a look inside, there are two tips to follow. First of all, measure the thickness: cavity-built walls, including those in a timber-framed construction, are usually about 280–295 mm (11–11½ in.) thick (including the thickness of the plaster, or plasterboard, on the inside); solid brick walls, up to two storeys in height, are usually about 230–250 mm (9–10 in.), but in taller buildings may be about 360 mm (14 in.) or more.

Secondly, look at the bonding of the brickwork: in cavity-built walls, where the outer leaf of brickwork is only about 110 mm (4¼ in.) thick, the bricks will have been laid in what is called a stretcher bond, i.e., all end to end; whereas in solid-built walls the bricks *should* (!) have been laid in a form of bonding where some bricks have been placed crosswise, through the thickness of the wall, these bricks being known as headers. There are various patterns of bonding *(see Figure 3)*.

If a brick wall is cement-rendered, or has some form of cladding on the outside, then there is no simple way of determining the bonding. Similarly, where walls are plastered on the inside, there is no simple way of determining the bonding or the materials of which the inner leaf is built, although you could try taking a look at the top of the wall if it is accessible inside the roof space. You can usu-

EXTERNAL WALLS

Brick bonding

Figure 3

'Stretcher' bond – the bricks are all laid lengthways

'Sussex' bond – 'headers' are laid across
the thickness of the wall

ally verify modern timber-framed construction, however, by first establishing that the wall is of cavity construction, and then by tapping the inside surfaces; a hollow sound in most areas indicates the likelihood of a timber-framed wall surfaced with plasterboard.

Don't be fooled; some forms of wall construction may not be all that they first appear. For example, there are many instances of cement-rendered walls where the cement rendering has been applied to expanded metal (like chicken wire, but with much smaller holes in the mesh) fixed to timber framing. Certain patterns of tile, when fixed vertically as a cladding, look just like brickwork. You may even find external walls which are only 100–150 mm (4–6 in.) thick – usually faced with an external cladding for weather resistance. In all cases, remember that the type of construction may vary around in different parts of the same building.

Make sure your walls are weather-resistant
As so many of the problems with external walls are caused by the weather, it is essential to check that your walls are weather-resistant. The following check-list will help you do this:

The joints in brickwork or stonework can become soft

EXTERNAL WALLS

and porous, and may need to be raked out and repointed.

Bricks and stones themselves can become excess-ively weathered (and porous) with age. Defective parts should be cut out and renewed or, if the wall is sufficiently sound, it may be possible to protect it with cement ren-dering or a suitable cladding – but make sure the win-dowsills still project far enough beyond the rendering to enable water to drip off without running down the face of the wall, and do not cover over any air bricks.

If the walls are cement-rendered, make sure there are no cracks where water can get behind the rendering; water which gets in will not only soak into the wall, but will also accelerate deterioration of the rendering. Cracked and loose rendering should be hacked off and renewed.

All types of external cladding need to be kept in a sound and weatherproof condition. Timber cladding, for example, should be kept well painted, and any rotten sections should be renewed at the earliest opportunity.

Where walls are of solid construction, make sure the outside ground level is at least 150 mm (6 in.) below the level of the damp-proof course; this will not only prevent the risk of rising dampness, but will also ensure that rain splashing up off the ground does not saturate the wall.

In timber-framed buildings, it is especially important to ensure the timber parts are protected from the inside, so that condensation does not get into the structure. Make sure the vapour barrier, built in during construction, does not get punctured in any way (if, for example, you are fix-ing shelves on the inside wall).

Finally, make quite sure that outside walls are not soaked by faulty rainwater gutters or downpipes, or other plumbing (externally or internally), or by poor design features, such as windowsills which do not project adequately.

Problems with walls
Problems usually manifest themselves as cracks or bulges, or in some kind of deterioration of the wall sur-face. Although surface defects can be put right by cos-

EXTERNAL WALLS

EXTERNAL WALLS

metic repairs, you should always try to discover the underlying reason for the problem.

Problems tend to result from one or more of the following:
- expansion and contraction (from variations in temperature or from the effects of moisture)
- alterations which have been carried out to the wall, or to the building (such as partly removed chimney breasts, or openings formed without adequate support above)
- deterioration of parts of the wall, invariably due to excessive moisture getting into the structure (such as timber built into the wall becoming rotten, metal within the wall becoming corroded, or natural deterioration of the materials of which the wall is built)
- inadequate strength or design
- poor construction (where the wall itself is not connected properly to the rest of the building)
- inadequate foundations, or problems in the ground beneath the foundations (such as frost affecting shallow foundations in chalky and sandy soil, or moisture causing swelling or shrinkage in clay soils)

WHAT TO LOOK OUT FOR

EXTERNAL WALLS

▶ **Symptom**
Bulging or cracking of the cement rendering on the outside walls.

▶ **Cause**
a Physical damage, e.g. vehicle impact.
b Incorrect mix of the cement rendering.
c Moisture getting in between the rendering and the wall.
d Frost action – resulting from moisture freezing behind the rendering.

e A defect in the wall structure to which the rendering is applied.

▶ **Remedy**
a–d If the rendering has bulged or cracked as a result of the rendering itself losing its key with the masonry behind it (i.e., the rendering is loose), but the wall itself is intact, the affected areas of rendering should be hacked off and replaced. The wall surface may first need to be made sound – e.g., by repairing any seriously unsound masonry and/or painting a stabilising solution onto powdery or dusty masonry.

Consider an alternative cladding material.

Above all, make sure no water can get behind the rendering or cladding.

e If the wall itself is unsound, see the next sections.

▶ **Symptom**
Bulging (in walls not surfaced with cement rendering).

▶ **Cause**
a Overloaded walls (inadequate thickness, poor construction or alterations carried out to the building).
b Rotting of timber built into the wall.
c Excess moisture or chemical attack – especially in exposed positions, e.g., gables or chimneys.
d Roof spread (*see Figure 4*).

Figure 4

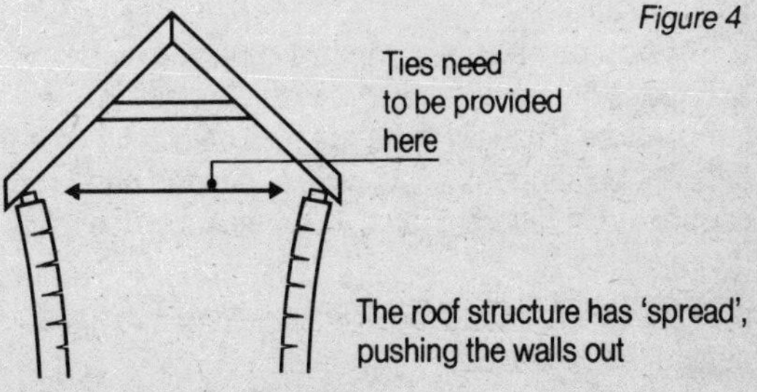

Ties need to be provided here

The roof structure has 'spread', pushing the walls out

EXTERNAL WALLS

EXTERNAL WALLS

e Inadequate horizontal restraint, e.g. where first floor joists run parallel to a long wall (*see Figure 5*).
f Chemical reactions within the structure.

Figure 5

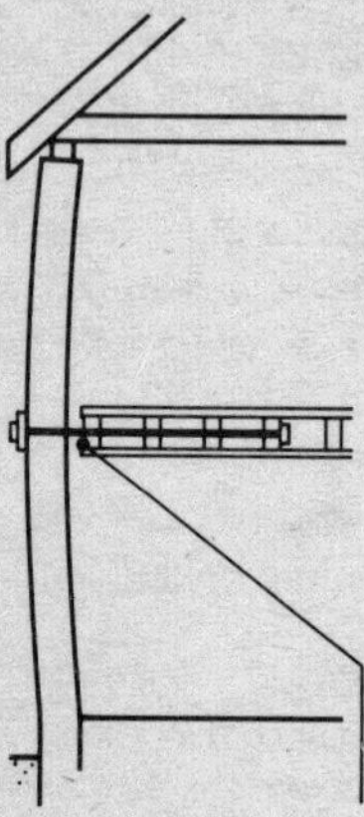

The side wall has bulged half-way up because the first floor joists are parallel to it and do not provide any support (or 'lateral restraint').
Ties can be built in at first floor level, fixed to the floor joists, if the wall is still reasonably stable.

Ties need to be built in at first floor level, fixed to the floor joists

▶ **Remedy**
Eliminate the cause of the bulging, then repair or rebuild those sections of the wall that have been affected. The effects of roof spread and inadequate horizontal restraint can be reduced by building in ties (*see Figures 4 and 5*). Professional advice should be obtained on the best course of action.

▶ **Symptom**
Cracking (in walls not surfaced with cement rendering).

▶ **Cause**
a Physical damage, e.g., vehicle impact.
b Expansion or contraction due to changes in temperature – usually there are hairline cracks where different building materials have expanded and contracted at different rates – or shrinkage due to drying out.
c Settlement in a new structure – usually there are

hairline cracks, and these are often found around the tops of windows and doors.

d Subsidence of the foundations, or 'heave' – normally occurs only if the foundations are shallow. (*See Figure 6.*)

Subsidence and clay 'heave'   *Figure 6*

Subsidence

Tree roots absorb moisture, causing clay to shrink. Building subsides.

Clay heave

Tree roots take up moisture

Tree felled so moisture not taken up

Clay absorbs moisture and expands, pushing building up

e Corrosion of ferrous materials – when metal becomes rusty it expands in volume, and rigid materials surrounding the metal (such as brickwork or concrete) will crack as a result of this.

f Poor design, or a result of later alterations made to the building.

▶ Remedy

Eliminate the cause of the cracking, if this is possible! If cracking is likely to occur, but within reasonable tolerances (e.g., thermal movement between dissimilar materials), then form an expansion joint filled with a flexible sealant, to keep the structure weathertight.

Cracking from subsidence may require the foundations to be underpinned in order to prevent a recurrence. Before repairing cracks caused by metal corrosion, expose the metal, remove all traces of corrosion and apply a rust-inhibiting solution (or replace the corroded metal).

Repair the damaged masonry when the cause of future cracking has been removed.

If in any doubt, obtain professional help for a diagnosis of the cause of the cracking and for advice on the correct remedy.

▶ Symptom

Surface discoloration created by a white powder, usually only found on new brickwork.

▶ Cause

Efflorescence, caused by salts in clay bricks, which can be aggravated by an ineffective damp-proof course.

▶ Remedy

It will wash away in time. It can be washed off using a hose if it is acute, or brushed off when the wall is dry. Ensure the damp-proof courses are effective.

▶ Symptom

Flaking or deterioration of masonry surfaces.

▶ Cause

a Excessive efflorescence in the bricks.

b Frost in brickwork or stonework (water getting into porous brickwork will later expand when freezing, causing the masonry to disintegrate).
c Vehicle impact.
d Excessive loading of the structure.
e Poor quality, or defective, masonry – or simply old age.

▶ **Remedy**
Determine the cause of the problem. If (**d**), get professional advice. Cut out and renew badly affected masonry. Prevent moisture getting into the masonry by checking and repairing (repointing) porous mortar joints. Check to ensure the damp-proof courses are effective.

▶ **Symptom**
a Bulging in timber on plastic cladding fixed to the outside walls.
b Defects in vertical tiling on the outside walls – broken tiles or tiles which have slipped out of place.

▶ **Cause**
a Inadequate allowance for thermal expansion, or swelling of the timber boarding.
b The tiles themselves may be defective. The fixing nails may have rusted, or the timber battens, to which the tiles are fixed, may have rotted.

▶ **Remedy**
a Reduce the lengths of individual boards or planks and use flexible sealant between the joints, or buy proprietary joints made for use with plastic cladding. This may well mean taking down much, if not all, of the cladding and starting again.
b Renew the tiles, fixing nails or battens. (See also the section on Roofs – Slates and Tiles, page 11.)

EXTERNAL WALLS

WINDOWS & DOORS

Windows and Doors

Get to know your windows and doors

Doors and windows are made of wood, metal or plastic, or may be a combination of these. Windows are generally one of two basic types: those with hinged casements (specially designed windows which can be built into sloping roofs are a variety of this type), or those with sliding sashes (*see Figure 7*). It is normal practice in the UK for window casements to open outwards, whereas in

Side-hung casement

Figure 7

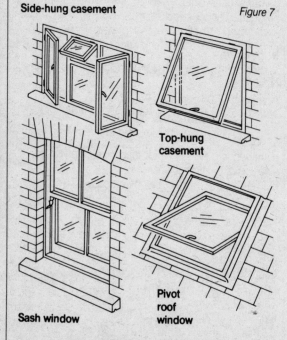

Top-hung casement

Sash window

Pivot roof window

some countries, particularly in the rest of Europe, casements open inwards (hence the reason for referring to full-height inward-opening casements as French windows). External doors, on the other hand, usually open inwards; they are invariably hinged, except in the case of modern, sliding patio doors.

In timber frames, glass is secured in place with putty (after initially fixing it in position with metal pins, known in the building trade as sprigs), or with timber beads (strips of timber of small cross section) or a combination of both. Obscure, patterned glass should be fixed with the textured face on the inside, where it is less likely to become coated with dirt. This is important where timber beads are used externally for fixing, because there is otherwise a greater risk of water getting between the beads and the glass.

In steel windows, glass is secured in place with putty, but, in modern aluminium or plastic windows, special rubber, or flexible plastic, gaskets are incorporated for this purpose.

In some instances, individual casements are divided into smaller panes with glazing bars, these invariably being made of the same material as the casement itself. True leaded lights consist of quite small pieces of glass (usually rectangular or diamond-shaped) held together by strips of lead, but some modern so-called leaded lights are really one piece of glass with lead strips stuck over the surface.

Glass is manufactured in a variety of qualities and thicknesses, including certain types which incorporate metal wire; when replacing broken panes you should go to a reputable glass merchant and get advice on the correct type for the size and location of the window or door. Fully glazed doors and low-level windows, for example, should be fitted with toughened or laminated glass. Windows and doors may be designed with sufficient space, or glazing rebate, to accept factory-made double-glazed units, in which two panes of glass are separated by a small gap and sealed at their edges.

The sashes in vertically sliding sash windows have to be prevented from sliding down (by gravity) when you

WINDOWS & DOORS

WINDOWS & DOORS

want to keep them open. In modern windows of this type, this is done by means of springs, or simply by friction between the sashes and the frame. But in older windows the sashes are counterbalanced by means of weights attached to sash cords. Here the sash cords are fixed to the sash itself and pass over pulleys in the top of the frame. Most of the mechanism is boxed in, out of sight. Every opening sash should have a sash cord on each side (*see Figure 8*).

Sash window   *Figure 8*

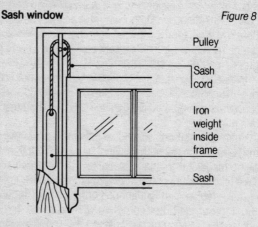

Pulley

Sash cord

Iron weight inside frame

Sash

Problems with windows and doors
Problems are mostly associated with excessive weathering, where there is inadequate paint on timber or steel units, or simply old age. Timber and steel, when in contact with the weather, are obviously susceptible to moisture and it is essential to keep them protected. Special care must be taken in the case of the end grain of timbers (such as the ends of projecting sills) where deterioration can take place rapidly. You should check that there is an adequate groove underneath projecting sills – to encourage water to drip off the sill instead of running back underneath towards the face of the wall, where it can accumulate and affect the joinery. Excessive internal condensation can lead to deterioration from the inside.

Rain can be prevented from getting in under doors by means of a weatherboard fixed to the outside face of the door, and by a water bar (a projecting strip of metal or plastic) embedded in the sill.

External doors should be 44 mm (1½ in.) thick, whereas internal doors normally have a thickness of only 32 mm (1¼ in.). Panels in external doors are often of plywood only 6 mm (¼ in.) thick, which, apart from being a security risk, can give rise to condensation on the inside and, in any case, is susceptible to early deterioration.

Careful attention needs to be paid to any joinery close to ground level, to make sure it does not become saturated by dampness from the ground. The lower parts of garage door frames are often affected in this way.

In the case of box frames of vertically sliding sash windows, where there are enclosed spaces out of sight, dry rot can occur unnoticed if moisture is allowed to get into the joinery.

Vertically sliding sash windows made of timber should always have pairs of handles fixed to the bottom rails of the sashes; without these, there is a tendency to pull down on the centre of the bottom rails when closing the window, with the consequent risk of damage to the timber joints and glazing. A problem with windows of this type is that they wear out with age: the sashes can become loose and will then rattle. The timber beads which hold the sashes in place can work loose or may split; their condition should be checked from time to time.

The chief problem with steel casement windows is that of corrosion, particularly in houses built in the 1930s, when the steel was not given a galvanised protective coating. Steel windows of a later date had the benefit of this process during manufacture. Corrosion has an expanding effect when it takes place and, in expanding, it puts pressure on the glass and ultimately causes it to crack. This seems to occur more frequently in windows divided into small panes with metal glazing bars. Hinges and window catches will break if corrosion is not retarded.

WINDOWS & DOORS

Modern aluminium and plastic frames are mostly free from problems of the types mentioned above. Non-anodised aluminium can discolour, showing a white powdery surface, due to a chemical reaction (oxidation), but may be cleaned with fine wire wool and/or metal polish.

Alterations
If you decide to alter the size of any windows or doors, make sure the wall above is properly supported. If you renew bay windows where there is another floor or roof above, do not take out any timbers which might be supporting the structure above.

Changing or renewing the glass in a vertically sliding sash window is likely to make the sash heavier and you may then have to open up the box frame to make the counterbalance weights heavier.

If you alter an existing door, or form a new door opening, make sure there is an effective and continuous damp-proof course below the frame. If the bottom of the frame is below the level of the existing damp-proof course, then make sure there is a vertical damp-proof course on each side of the frame – so that the realigned damp-proof course is continuous.

When altering window sizes (or if windows have already been altered) remember that for adequate ventilation you should retain *opening* windows with an area, or total area, of at least one-twentieth of the floor area of the room.

WHAT TO LOOK OUT FOR

CASEMENT WINDOWS AND DOORS

▶ **Symptom**
Gaps at corner joints or rot in the timber. Glass cracked across the corners of panes in steel units.

34

Glazing putty that is cracked or loose.

▶ Cause
Water penetration could be causing swelling or deterioration of the timber, or corrosion in steel. This is invariably due to inadequate paint cover.

▶ Remedy
a Timber units – make sure the timber is sound. Replace, or piece-in, new sections of timber. Clean off any cracked and flaking paint. Prime the bare timber. Fill cracks and gaps. Cut out and renew cracked or loose sections of glazing putty. Prime again and paint with undercoat and gloss paint (two undercoats on external faces).
Note: If the deterioration is excessive, it is sometimes less expensive to replace a complete casement, or even the entire frame, than to replace small pieces.
b Steel units – thoroughly clean the metal parts, using a wire brush (remove the glass if necessary). Treat the bare metal with a proprietary rust inhibitor and/or metal primer. Renew the broken glass. Paint with undercoat and gloss paint (two undercoats on external faces). Make sure all hinges and catches work properly and apply a few drops of lubricating oil to these.
c All types – check the underside of the sill to ensure water does not run back underneath. Clean out the groove or cut a new groove to form a drip.

TIMBER SASH WINDOWS

▶ Symptom
a Sashes that are too heavy to lift, or won't stay open.
b Loose glass.
c Sashes that jam, or are stiff to operate.
d See the problems affecting casement windows.

WINDOWS & DOORS

WINDOWS & DOORS

▶ Cause
a A broken sash cord or a pulley that is not running freely. The counterbalance weights could be of incorrect size or weight, because modern glass is heavier than original glass.
b Defective joint(s) between the glazing bar(s) and the horizontal rails of the sash.
c The timber beads, which hold the sashes in alignment, may be loose or broken.

▶ Remedy
a Renew the sash cords. Lubricate the pulleys. Adjust the counterbalance weights.
b Repair or renew the joint(s) between the glazing bar(s) and the bottom rail.
c Check the condition of the beads which keep the sashes in alignment, and repair or renew these as necessary. Apply candlewax to lubricate the timber surfaces which are in contact with each other.

DOORS

▶ Symptom
Rain blowing in underneath the door.

▶ Cause
Rain runs down the face of the door and back underneath, instead of dripping off the front.

▶ Remedy
a Fit a weatherboard (with a groove underneath) to the face of the door.
b Fit a metal, or hard plastic, water bar, or securely fix a hardwood strip (with screws and glue) into the sill underneath the door.

Note: This requires a rebate to be cut along the bottom edge of the door. To do this, the door has to be taken off its hinges.

Gutters and Downpipes

Get to know your gutters and downpipes

Eave gutters are normally made of cast iron, zinc, asbestos-cement, or plastic. The downpipes to which they connect are usually of the same materials, but you may find that gutters have been renewed in plastic, for example, while the original cast-iron downpipes still remain.

Most houses and bungalows have downpipes on the outside of the building; large blocks of flats sometimes have downpipes located inside, boxed-in and out of sight. Older properties may have valley or parapet gutters (around the perimeter of the building), and these are usually lined with lead or zinc. It is especially important to keep valley and parapet gutters in good condition, as any leakages will almost certainly let water into the building. In any event, rainwater should always be prevented from running down, or saturating, the walls.

The most common failings in gutters and downpipes result from a lack of routine maintenance. Inadequate paint on cast-iron fittings leads to premature corrosion: unless the inside surfaces of metal gutters are fully coated with bituminous paint, water which does not drain away quickly will have a harmful effect. Some old cast-iron gutters have wooden stop ends, and these are frequently found to be in poor condition. A blockage which is allowed to build up at the base of a metal downpipe will accelerate corrosion; and if water in a blocked downpipe then freezes, it is quite likely to expand and split the pipe, and saturate the wall to which the pipe is fixed.

Downpipes which connect directly to underground drains (instead of discharging over gulley gratings) are more likely to suffer from these problems – and access for clearing blockages is obviously restricted.

You can prevent leaves and silt from getting into, and possibly blocking, the downpipes by fitting wire or plastic balloons in the gutter outlets. A build-up of leaves in the gutter will then cause the gutter to overflow, but you will at least be able to get at, and clear, the blockage, which you would not be able to do so easily if the blockage had occurred inside a downpipe.

Plastic fittings are relatively trouble-free, except from physical damage to exposed downpipes. Some of the plastic fittings, first produced some years ago, tend to become quite brittle with age, although modern techniques seem to have overcome this problem.

Where roof coverings are underfelted, the underfelt should ideally project into the gutters to minimise the risk of rainwater running down the face of the wall instead of into the gutter. Do not be tempted to cut off any underfelt which projects in this way!

WHAT TO LOOK OUT FOR

GUTTERS AND DOWNPIPES

▶ **Symptom**
The gutter is overflowing or leaking.

▶ **Cause**
a Blockage.
b Insufficient slope of gutter, or defective gutter brackets.
c Not enough downpipes.
d Defective gutter, gutter joints or fittings.

▶ **Remedy**
a Clear out the gutter.
b Realign the gutter, and check and replace the gutter brackets.
c Provide additional downpipes.
d Repair or replace the gutter, gutter joints, stop ends, etc.

▶ **Symptom**
The downpipe is leaking.

▶ **Cause**
a The downpipe is split, or it is blocked and
overflowing at a joint.

▶ **Remedy**
Clear out any blockage in the pipe. Check whether
the drain is blocked. Repair or replace the downpipe.

Drainage

Get to know your pipes and drains

Soil pipes are those which serve water closets or toilets;
all other sanitary and kitchen appliances connect to
waste pipes. In relatively modern properties bathroom
waste pipes usually then connect to a single (soil and
waste) pipe. In older properties, especially in blocks of
flats, there is usually one pipe above ground level for soil
drainage and a separate one for waste water. In some
properties all of these pipes are inside the building, invariably boxed in out of sight, but in most properties, especially those more than 20 years old, the soil and waste
pipes are fixed externally.

   Soil pipes were, at one time, always made of lead, then
cast iron was used extensively, and nowadays they are
most often made of plastic. Asbestos-cement pipes have
also been used. Smaller-diameter waste pipes are of the
same materials, although copper and steel pipes have
been used over the past 40 years or so.

   Waste pipes from fittings at upper floor levels sometimes discharge into a hopper, fixed externally, with a
single pipe down to ground level, which then discharges
over a waste water gulley. The gulley is in turn connected

DRAINAGE

DRAINAGE

to the underground drainage system.

Soil and waste water is disposed of by means of underground drains connected to the public sewerage system (*see Figure 9*) or, in older properties or rural areas, to a cesspool or septic tank. A cesspool is a large, watertight underground chamber, usually built of brickwork and covered with a concrete slab, which has to be pumped out periodically into a mobile tanker to prevent it from overflowing. A septic tank is similar to a cesspool, but consists of two or more interconnected chambers, operating like a miniature sewage works and with land drain outlets, so that it does not normally need pumping out. It is possible to connect rainwater to the same (soil and waste water) drainage system but that system is then likely to become overloaded in times of heavy rainfall. For this reason, some local authorities insist that rainwater is not connected to the soil drains. It is better, therefore, to connect rainwater drains to separate soakaways – provided that the subsoil is of a type that does not easily become waterlogged. Soil and waste water must never be connected directly to a soakaway, of course, because of the obvious health hazard. Soakaways should always be located at least 5 m (15 ft) from the building so as not to affect the walls and foundations.

Underground drains have traditionally been constructed with clay or concrete pipes, with their joints rigidly sealed with cement mortar, or with cast-iron or pitch-fibre (a bituminous compound) pipes, but plastic pipes are now in common use.

Inspection chambers have to be provided for access to the drains for maintenance purposes; there should always be an inspection chamber at every change of direction of the drain (at the corners of buidings, for example). Inspection chambers have normally been built of brickwork (sometimes cement-rendered inside), but pre-formed interlocking concrete sections have been used in recent years and all-plastic inspection chambers are now becoming common.

It was, at one time, usual practice for there to be an interceptor trap (a water-sealed trap, similar to a gulley) in

Typical drainage layout *Figure 9*

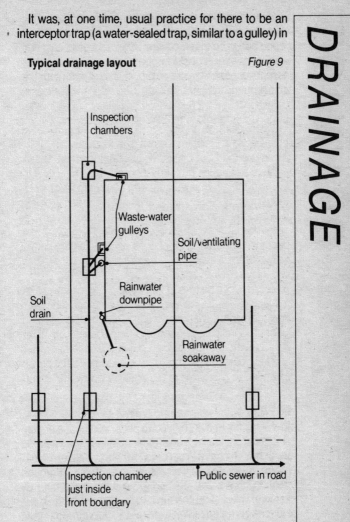

the inspection chamber nearest to the public sewer – the intention being to restrict smells from the public sewer from getting into the house drains. In such an instance, a fresh air inlet would be connected to the inspection chamber. Interceptor traps and fresh air inlet pipes of this type are rarely found in modern properties, however.

Inspection chamber covers, which can be of cast iron, steel or concrete, should not be covered over but must remain accessible. You can prevent metal covers rusting to their metal frames by coating the edges with grease.

Problems with soil and waste pipes

Physical damage can occur to pipes fixed outside the building, especially in driveways, and particularly if the pipes are made of plastic or asbestos cement. Plastic waste pipes, when run almost horizontally, may eventually sag if inadequately supported, and blockages may then occur. Sufficient fixing clips will avoid this problem. It is important to ensure that pipes fixed to the outside walls do not leak, otherwise the walls themselves can become saturated. If blockages occur in cold weather, water trapped inside may freeze and crack the pipes, especially old iron ones.

Hoppers can be a source of trouble, being susceptible to blockages from leaves, etc., and water can then overflow, damaging the wall to which the hopper is fixed. Hoppers should be cleaned out at least once a year. Similar problems can occur with gulley gratings becoming blocked, but this nuisance can be alleviated if the pipe is extended to discharge into the gulley below the level of the grating.

Problems with underground drains

Problems are usually related to physical damage or general deterioration with age. Pipes can become fractured by slight settlement in buildings (where drains run underneath), by excessive weights (such as traffic) at ground level, by tree roots growing around the pipes, and by freezing if water builds up in blocked pipes. It is not uncommon for rats to gnaw their way through pitch-fibre pipes. It is because of these drawbacks that plastic pipes with flexible couplings seem to have proved more reliable and are now used extensively.

If pipes become fractured, or if joints are not entirely

watertight, roots from nearby trees and bushes may find their way into the pipes, causing effluent to build up and ultimately create a blockage.

When drains are first constructed, they should be laid to an adequate gradient, but this sometimes is not the case and slow-moving or static effluent (especially grease from the kitchen) can then clog the pipes.

A problem with very old properties is that inspection chambers may have been permanently covered over, or there may not have been any inspection chambers in the first place. In these instances it is virtually impossible to find out whether a problem exists in the pipes – at least until the drains cease to work at all!

Inspection chambers can suffer from subsidence, but problems tend to relate to defects in the bricks of which the chambers are built and/or to defects in the cement rendering on the inside. Defective bricks, or cracked or loose rendering should always be replaced as soon as possible, before pieces fall off and block the drain. Inspection chamber covers can become corroded or broken, with breakages most likely to occur in a driveway where the cover is of insufficient strength. Cracked or broken covers should be replaced immediately to avoid the risk of personal injury.

WHAT TO LOOK OUT FOR

DRAINS

▶ **Symptom**
A blocked drain (the water not running away through the underground drain).

▶ **Cause**
a A build-up of grease or other solid matter in the interceptor trap, inside the inspection chambers, or in the drain between inspection chambers. Cement or concrete can get washed into the drains when building work is carried out.

DRAINAGE

DRAINAGE

b Tree roots in the pipes.
c An underground pipe may have broken, blocking the drain.
d The main sewer may be blocked (outside your property). A cesspool or septic tank may be blocked or full.

▶ **Remedy**

Start at the point furthest away from the house. This will reveal whether or not the problem is within your property. If it is not, contact your local council offices.

Lift the covers on the inspection chambers – but be careful not to let children or animals fall in! . Check the interceptor trap (if one exists), and locate the blockage.

If it is visible from within an inspection chamber, you may be able to remove the blockage using a stick (carefully – so as not to damage the drain pipes).

If you cannot pinpoint the blockage from within any inspection chamber, get a local builder, or drain-clearing specialist, to push drain rods through the pipes.

If there is a build-up of grease or other sediment in the drains, consider having them cleaned using high-pressure water-jets – normally carried out only by specialist drain-clearing companies.

Caution: Some drain-clearing specialists may offer to carry out a CCTV (closed circuit television) survey of the inside of the drain, using a special camera and video equipment. This can be expensive and is not normally necessary unless you need to confirm that a pipe is cracked or broken. Ask about the costs of drain clearing, water jetting or CCTV surveys before you engage any such firm, and do not be persuaded to have any specialist work done unless you are convinced it is essential.

If you have reason to suspect a pipe is broken, tell your house insurers before you incur any costs. Your house insurance policy may well cover the cost of a CCTV survey and subsequent repairs for damage to underground pipes – provided you first obtain agreement from your insurers on the course of action to be taken.

Pavings

Get to know your pavings

The area immediately surrounding your property, like a moat around a castle, is all-important in protecting your home. You need to ensure that the soil and pavings, drains and airbricks in this vital area are not neglected.

As stated elsewhere, the ground level immediately outside should be at least 150 mm (6 in.) below the level of the damp-proof course to avoid the risk of rising dampness. If you cannot find a damp-proof course in the wall, the ground level should be at least 200 mm (8 in.) below the level of the ground floor.

It is not uncommon for paths and drives to be built up over the years and ultimately finish up at, or even above, the level of the damp-proof course. Paths and pavings may even have been laid sloping towards the wall, or the pavings may have subsided so as to slope towards the wall, with the result that water will pond against the wall instead of draining away. Make sure, of course, that there are no flower beds or heaps of earth built up to, or above, the damp-proof course.

If the general slope of the ground is towards the wall, the soil should be cut back at an angle of 45 degrees and a paved area formed, tilting back from the wall towards the soil (*see Figure 10*).

Where paths and drives close to the building exceed just a few square metres in area, try to achieve proper

PAVINGS

Correct position of paving next to external wall

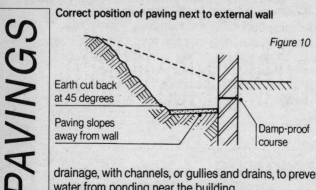

Figure 10

Earth cut back at 45 degrees

Paving slopes away from wall

Damp-proof course

drainage, with channels, or gullies and drains, to prevent water from ponding near the building.

Rainwater downpipes should never be allowed simply to discharge water onto the ground next to the walls; they should always terminate over gullies – with a small kerb around the gulley grating to ensure that all water flows into the gulley. The space around the edge of the gulley itself should be kept watertight by pointing up with cement mortar. Kerbs and pointing around gullies can deteriorate quickly with age and should be repaired to prevent concentrations of water from seeping into the ground next to the wall.

Airbricks or metal ventilators in the outside walls close to ground level will almost certainly have been provided for ventilating the space under a timber-built ground floor and these must always be kept clear. An accumulation of paint, dirt, or plant growth can easily block up a ventilation opening of this type, thus increasing the possibility of rot in the ground floor timbers. Insulation injected into a cavity-built wall can also block ventilation openings in certain circumstances; use a screwdriver or a similar tool to check that they are clear if you have had your walls insulated.

The Enemies Within

This section of the book investigates some of the more serious complaints from which your house can suffer. The symptoms appear inside, but often result from causes outside.

It is normally best for these particular problems to be dealt with by specialist contractors, who usually carry out investigations and give estimates free of charge. In most cases, these contractors guarantee the work which they carry out – but they do not normally guarantee that similar problems will not occur elsewhere in the house. You *must* keep an accurate record of those areas of the house in which specialist treatment or repairs have been undertaken, so that you will know whether or not any recurrence of the problem is in an area to which a guarantee applies. You should ensure that the contractor supplies a plan which identifies the work undertaken, and this should be attached to any written guarantee.

The usefulness of a guarantee depends, of course, on the contractor remaining in business. You may be able to purchase an 'insurance' policy to cover the eventuality of the contractor closing down; some contractors themselves contribute to schemes of this sort.

You can get advice on these points, and on the standard of work which you can expect from contractors, from a chartered surveyor; a surveyor can also be asked to check that the repairs recommended by the contractor are appropriate and sufficient – but you will almost certainly have to pay for this service.

Rising Damp

WHAT TO LOOK OUT FOR

RISING DAMP

▶ **Symptom**

Damp areas showing on walls, fairly close to ground level.

▶ **Cause**

Dampness from the ground rising up the wall by capillary action through porous building materials, such as brickwork. The rising moisture tends to carry salts from the ground into the masonry, and the salts then collect and crystallise with the internal wall plaster. These salts will themselves absorb airborne moisture and give a damp appearance – independent of any dampness within the wall.

External walls are most likely to become affected, but internal and party walls can also suffer if there is no effective damp-proof course.

Rising damp can occur where there is no damp-proof course or where an otherwise effective damp-proof course has been damaged, or has become 'bridged'. For further details, see the section which looks at problems with external walls (page 20).

▶ **Remedy**

Check to see whether the outside ground level is at least 150 mm (6 in.) below an existing damp-proof course – recognised by a thin layer of bitumen (tar) or bituminous felt (like roofing felt), or a double layer of slates, set in a horizontal brick joint around the building. Reduce the ground level or clear away earth or debris as necessary.

In an older house, the damp-proof course may no longer be effective, or there may be no damp-proof

Roof maintenance is vital, as leaks cause structural
damage and electrical hazards (see pages 8 and 135).

Rising damp will damage wall plaster, causing wallpaper to peel; it can also lead to rotting floor timbers (see page 48).

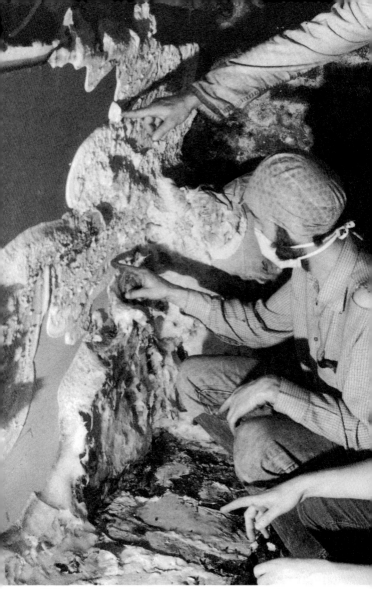

This cellar shows the effects of dry rot – your home's worst enemy (see page 51).

Wet rot is caused by timber being in contact with a very damp wall (see page 52).

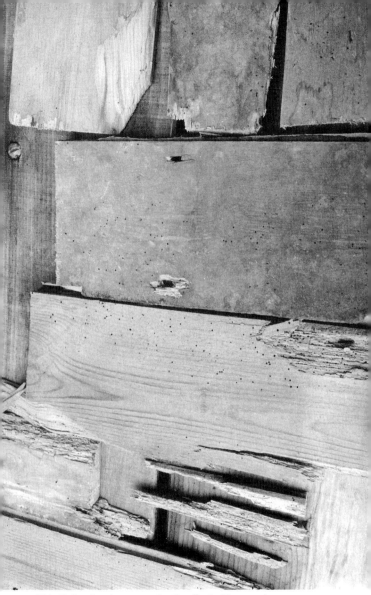
This timber has been very badly affected by woodworm,
which can lead to structural problems (see page 53).

Condensation is often a problem in poorly ventilated rooms (see page 55).

Cracks sometimes occur in internal walls that are not properly bonded to solid external walls (see page 65).

This light switch should have been replaced long ago -
don't rely on damaged electrical fittings (see page 121).

course at all; in either of these cases, a horizontal barrier (new damp-proof course) must be installed at least 150 mm (6 in.) above the adjoining ground level. There may also be a need for vertical damp-proof courses at the ends of horizontal sections, in order to form a waterproof barrier between your walls and others which might remain damp, such as neighbouring walls or garden walls.

A new damp-proof course can be put into existing walls by cutting the brickwork and inserting an impervious material; by inserting porous tubes; by a system called electro-osmosis; or by injecting, or transfusing, a water-repellent resin into the masonry.

The installation of a new damp-proof course normally has to be done by a specialist firm, who would give a 20- or 30-year written guarantee. This guarantee is usually valid only if specified conditions are met – for example, salt-contaminated plaster must be renewed. The correct materials must be used when replastering is carried out. Specialist firms may do this work themselves, or may specify the materials to be used. Modern quick-setting lightweight plaster, such as Carlite, must be avoided.

Penetrating Damp

WHAT TO LOOK OUT FOR

PENETRATING DAMP

▶ **Symptom**
Damp patches on the walls – not necessarily near ground level. Sometimes they are on chimney

PENETRATING DAMP

breasts, especially just below roof level.

▶ **Cause**

Moisture penetrating the outer fabric of the building. Porous brickwork, or brick joints, will let rainwater through a solid wall, as will cracked cement rendering, or any other kind of defective facing on the outside of the wall. Defective brickwork, or ineffective flashings between the roof covering and a chimney stack above roof level, can also be the reason for dampness getting in.

▶ **Remedy**

For dampness on external walls, check the condition of the bricks and, more important, the soundness of the mortar joints. Repair or repoint as necessary. If the outside of the wall is cement-rendered, check this for cracks and soundness. Check external claddings, such as vertical tiling or timber boarding, for cracks and gaps, and repair as necessary.

For dampness on chimney breasts, check the condition of the chimney stack brickwork and mortar joints, and the condition of the flashings between the roof covering and the chimney stack; you will probably have to use a pair of binoculars to do this. Metal flashings are also used to form a weathertight joint at the perimeter of some kinds of roof structures. Flashings can become loose, leaving gaps, or can split or corrode with age. Check also the condition of the roof covering itself and make sure there are no gaps where the rain can get in. (See the sections which look at problems with roofs and chimneys, pages 8–19.)

Dry Rot

WHAT TO LOOK OUT FOR

DRY ROT

▶ **Symptom**

Fungus on timber which, initially, looks like cotton wool, but later turns grey or yellow and then a rusty red colour. It smells of mushrooms. Its rate of spread is typically up to 1 m (3 ft) a year; grey strands extend behind plaster and through porous brickwork in search of timber on which the fungus can grow. Affected timber, usually hidden from view, has distinctive 'cubical' cracking and crumbles into powder.

▶ **Cause**

Timber becoming moist (but not wet) in a medium-cool and poorly ventilated environment allows the spores of dry rot fungus to thrive. The spores are in the air in all urban areas. Spaces under timber ground floors are often affected because suitably moist conditions can occur in these areas. Timber beams, panelling and window frames in contact with damp walls are also susceptible.

▶ **Remedy**

The cause of the moisture must be eliminated. Affected timber cannot be treated and must be taken out of the building and burned; all timber within 300–400 mm (12″–16″) of the visible strands of the fungus must be dealt with in this way. Replacement timber should be of a type which has been pressure-impregnated with preservative. Masonry adjoining affected timber can be sterilised by chemical injection. This work is best carried out by a specialist firm, who would normally give a 30-year written guarantee in respect of the areas treated.

Dry rot fungus can be malignant and may re-appear if moist conditions persist.

WET ROT

Wet Rot

WHAT TO LOOK OUT FOR

WET ROT

▶ **Symptom**
Thread-like strands, usually brown or black, extending over timber (and adjacent masonry), sometimes with small growths of yellow/brown coloured 'fingers'. Usually only found where there is no daylight. The affected timber wrinkles and cracks along the grain, and loses all strength by literally rotting away.

▶ **Cause**
Timber becoming wet – often where plumbing and drainage leaks occur at or below ground level – if the damp-proof course is ineffective, for example.

▶ **Remedy**
The cause of dampness must be eliminated and affected timber must be replaced. Work can be undertaken by a reputable general builder or specialist firm.

Wet rot will only persist while timber is wet and will cease to be a problem once the dampness has been eliminated.

Woodworm

WHAT TO LOOK OUT FOR

WOODWORM

▶ **Symptom**

Small holes in timber (about 1.5–4 mm in diameter), usually in floor boards or roof timbers, but often underneath stairs, and particularly in plywood. These flight holes, as they are called, are caused by beetles gnawing their way out of the timber – after the beetle larvae have bored their way around inside the timber (sometimes for several years).

A number of different beetles affect timber in this way. The most common is the Common Furniture Beetle. Death Watch Beetle and, less frequently, House Longhorn Beetle (found almost only in the southern home counties of England) have long life-cycles and can cause extensive structural damage.

▶ **Cause**

The larvae of the insects hatch out and thrive in the timber. Old, already affected furniture, put in roof spaces or cupboards, is often the cause of a large-scale attack by the Common Furniture Beetle.

▶ **Remedy**

Chemical spraying or coating of the affected timber. This is best done by a reputable firm specialising in this kind of work. Usually it is not a particularly expensive operation, and precautionary treatment can also be carried out on unaffected timber. Most specialist firms give a 30-year written guarantee against further infestation of those timbers which they have treated.

WOODWORM

Looking for woodworm

The places where you are most likely to find Common Furniture Beetle are:

In the roof

around the access hatch – where it is likely to be the warmest spot (woodworm like to be cosy); or at the eaves – where the beetles might have flown in from another property.

In the floors

around water closets – where woodworm grubs will thrive on the protein in urine-soaked floorboards (an unpleasant thought, but true), and where old furniture at one time might have stood – in front of windows where chests or tables might have been situated. Also near ventilation openings under the ground floor.

In the cupboards (and in garages and sheds)

anywhere that old furniture might have been stored (remember, the Common Furniture Beetle tends to live in old furniture). Under the stairs is a typical location, and especially where plywood panelling exists (the grubs will thrive on the protein in certain kinds of glue used for laminating plywood).

NOTE: Although Common Furniture Beetle is the kind found most frequently, there are many other species of 'woodworm' – and they could be found in almost any part of the building.

Condensation

WHAT TO LOOK OUT FOR

CONDENSATION

This is something you can deal with yourself – unlike the problems mentioned above, it does not normally need to be dealt with by a specialist contractor.

▶ **Symptom**
Steamed-up windows, damp walls and ceilings (and sometimes floors) which, if left in a moist condition, will attract mould growth – sometimes referred to as 'black spots'. Mould growth resulting from condensation is most likely to occur where there is little air movement – e.g. behind bulky furniture, in unventilated cupboards and poorly ventilated larders.

▶ **Cause**
Condensation occurs as a result of a fall in the temperature of the air. The atmosphere then has less capacity to hold water vapour, so it condenses on the coldest surfaces in the form of water droplets. Condensation is caused by cooking, washing and other household activities which involve the use of water or steam, and even the air we breathe out. This is how much water vapour is produced by:

Bath or shower	1 l (1¾ pt)
Family of five asleep at night	1.2 l (2 pt)
Two adults active for 16 hours	1.5 l (2½ pt)
One machine load of washing	2 l (3½ pt)
Cooking, per day	2.5 l (4½ pt)
Tumble drier, full load	4.2 l (7½ pt)
Paraffin (or gas) heater	1 l (1¾ pt) per litre of fuel
Indoor plants, etc.	even more

... and it's all got to go somewhere!

CONDENSATION

▶ Remedy

A good rule for bathrooms and kitchens is *'shut up and open up'*; in other words, shut the door and open the window in a room where you are creating steam. Fit a simple door spring if you like, but stop the steam, or moisture, getting into the rest of your home. It is most important to get the water vapour out of the building, and leaving a window open for half an hour after you have created the moisture is the cheapest solution.

Fitting an electric extractor fan might be more convenient. This can be installed in the window or in an outside wall. The best position is on the opposite side of the room to the point where fresh air can be drawn in. This will achieve a good cross-flow of air from one side of the room to the other. To save you the trouble of turning on the fan every time moisture is generated, you can install a humidistat – which is like a thermostat, but switches on whenever the humidity (rather than the temperature) rises above a pre-set limit. Some well-known manufacturers of extractor fans supply humidistats as an optional extra to the fan itself, or you can get a fan unit with a built-in humidistat.

An alternative method of ridding your home of water vapour is to install a fan which blows relatively dry air *in*, thus forcing moist air *out*. In other words, air is forced out where draughts would otherwise come in! One firm manufactures a small fan unit, which you install in your roof space, for forcing air into the house; this unit can be left switched on permanently as it operates automatically by means of a thermostat – turning itself off in summer when condensation is not normally a problem.

A special kind of unit is now available, which consists of two interconnected fans – one extracting air and one blowing fresh air in. A heat exchanger element ensures that the cold air coming in is heated by the warm air going out; thus there is an effective change of air with minimal heat loss. These units are available in a range of sizes to suit different needs.

Small dehumidifiers, which contain moisture-absorbing chemical crystals, are advertised in the press and can be bought in DIY shops. They may be adequate for small areas, such as inside wardrobes – if this is where you have a condensation problem – but they are unlikely to be suitable for absorbing large volumes of water vapour.

Electric dehumidifiers are not yet commonplace but are likely to become so within the next few years as we draughtproof and seal up our homes so that water vapour cannot escape. These physically extract water from the atmosphere by means of a fan which draws in the air and blows it out through a condenser. Many such dehumidifiers have automatic humidistat control, and so can be left switched on. Condensed water is collected in a removable container, which can be emptied every two or three days. These dehumidifiers are an effective way of eliminating condensation problems – particularly if you do not want to open the windows. They are available in a range of operating capacities, but domestic models cost about the same as a colour TV: the running costs are equivalent to running three light bulbs.

Note: Condensation can also occur within the structure of a building – for example, inside chimney flues or roof spaces. Technically, this is known as 'interstitial condensation'. It occurs usually because that hidden space is both cold and poorly ventilated, causing any water vapour there to condense. These problems are referred to on pages 60 and 72.

CONDENSATION

Inside your House

The Roof Space

Get to know your roof space

Pitched, or sloping, roofs have traditionally been constructed with sets of timbers spaced apart – each set usually in the shape of a triangle, the tops of the pairs of rafters being connected with a ridge board. The slope, or pitch, of a roof is normally governed by the type of outer covering: plain tiles, for example, should be fixed at a steeper pitch than interlocking concrete tiles, to avoid the risk of rainwater running back underneath the tiles themselves. The sloping timbers, known as rafters, may need to be supported at an intermediate point to prevent them sagging and, for this reason, horizontal beams, known as purlins, are commonly found half-way up the slope of the rafters. The purlins are normally braced with struts, again forming a triangular shape for strength, and these can, additionally, be supported on gable end walls (*see Figure 11*).

The lower ends of each pair of rafters are normally held together by ceiling joists, to which the ceiling underneath is fixed, and these joists are sometimes braced apart by binders, fixed over the tops of the joists.

Alternatively, to prevent the rafters from spreading apart, or sometimes in addition to the ceiling joists, col-

Conventional roof construction

Figure 11

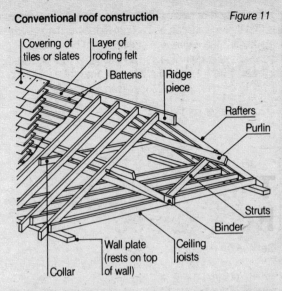

Covering of tiles or slates

Layer of roofing felt

Battens

Ridge piece

Rafters

Purlin

Struts

Binder

Wall plate (rests on top of wall)

Ceiling joists

Collar

lars are fixed between the rafters at a higher level. The whole structure is secured to timber wall plates, which are bedded in cement mortar on top of the supporting walls.

Some roofs are constructed with trusses every two or three metres apart, with rafters in between. The trusses are either of much larger timbers than would otherwise be the case, of pairs of timbers bolted together, or sometimes of steelwork, giving support to the purlins, and hence to the intermediate rafters.

Where a number of roof structures are of the same design, such as on housing estates, it has been common practice, over the last 30 years or so, for roofs to be built with what are known as trussed rafters. In this instance, the pairs of rafters, together with their corresponding ceiling joists, are fully braced as composite triangular units, not needing the addition of purlins or further struts. Trussed rafter units are prefabricated in a factory, with the individual timbers in each unit being fixed together with plywood or metal plates. The advantage to builders is that these units can be brought to the building, ready-made, and the entire roof structure can be erected and covered quite quickly. It is essential, in a roof built with trussed rafters, not to interfere with any of the individual timbers or their special fixings (*see Figure 12*).

Trussed rafter construction

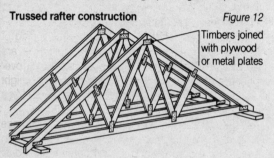

Figure 12

Timbers joined with plywood or metal plates

Roof structure problems

Roof spaces, especially those which have been made colder by the addition of insulation, should be well venti-lated to prevent an accumulation of water vapour inside. This applies to flat roofs as well as pitched roofs and is, nowadays, a mandatory requirement of the Building Regulations. Water vapour created within the house is likely to find its way into the roof and you need to provide a good draught across the roof space to expel any mois-ture, which could otherwise have an adverse effect on the timbers. If you install roof insulation where there was none before, or if you improve on existing roof insulation, do make sure the roof space is adequately ventilated. A number of firms manufacture fittings designed specifi-cally for roof-space ventilation and these fittings can be readily obtained from builders' merchants.

Whatever kind of roof structure you have in your own home it is important not to put any heavy weights inside the roof space, because the joists are normally of a size designed to take account *only* of the weight of the ceiling

THE ROOF SPACE

fixed underneath, and not of any additional loads. If some kind of boarding has been put down for access purposes, to prevent you from putting your foot through the ceiling below, it may be convenient to store lightweight objects, such as empty cardboard cartons, up here. But, even if the boarding looks strong enough, it is possible that the ceiling joists will bend and, although they may not break, the ceiling underneath might crack.

The same consideration goes for the positioning of cold-water storage cisterns which, when full of water, are quite heavy. These should always be positioned over supporting walls or, if this is not possible, their weight should be distributed, by means of timber beams, over a number of ceiling joists, instead of just two or three.

Never be tempted to cut out timbers in the roof space just because they might be in the way. They have been put there for a purpose and should only be altered or moved if you have obtained professional advice on the structure. Loft conversions have to be carefully designed and should never be attempted without first obtaining professional advice (and Building Regulations approval from the local authority).

THE ROOF SPACE

WHAT TO LOOK OUT FOR

ROOF SPACE

▶ **Symptom**
Dampness on the timbers.

▶ **Cause**
a Leaks in the roof.
b Condensation. (This can result from water vapour in the house or from steam coming out of the central heating expansion pipe.)

▶ **Remedy**
a Check the condition of the underfelt. Check and

THE ROOF SPACE

replace any defective slates or tiles. Check the condition of the fixing nails in the slates or tiles. Check the flashings adjoining the chimney stacks and the adjoining walls.

b Ventilate the roof space (see Chapter 2 – Enemies Within) by forming openings at eave level, installing air bricks in gable walls, or installing special ventilating tiles or ridge tiles. If steam is coming out of the central heating expansion pipe, check the boiler thermostat.

ROOF SPACE

▶ **Symptom**
Apparent bowing (or bending) of rafters or purlins.

▶ **Cause**
a Excessive weight of the roof covering (perhaps if slates have been replaced with tiles).
b Defects in the roof timbers.
c The original supporting timbers (e.g., struts and/or collars) having been removed.

▶ **Remedy**
Seek professional advice. It may be possible to install additional timbers, but care will be needed to ensure that the supporting walls are able to carry any additional weight.

Ceilings

Get to know your ceilings

In most properties built before about 1940, ceilings were of lath and plaster. In this form of construction, timber laths (thin strips of timber, about 25 mm (1 in.) wide) were nailed underneath ceiling joists and spaced about 5 mm apart. Plaster was then applied to the underside of the laths and this held itself in place by squeezing through the gaps while soft and projected over the top side of the laths. It then dried hard and 'held'.

In the last 50 years, however, ceilings have invariably been formed by the use of plasterboard, which is manufactured in panels of various sizes, usually 9 mm (⅜ in.) or 12 mm (½ in.) thick, comprising a sheet of rigid plaster with a heavy-duty paper lining on both sides. These panels are simply nailed to the underside of the ceiling joists, and the joints are then filled with plaster. Plasterboard panels may sometimes be given a thin plaster coat or a decorative (textured) finish, or may simply be decorated direct with either paint or a heavy-duty lining paper.

Problems with ceilings

Problems are indicated mostly by cracked and/or loose plaster. In recently built properties hairline cracks can occur as a result of shrinkage (i.e., drying out), as is often the case at the junction between the ceiling and the walls. These cracks can be filled, or masked, by fitting a plaster cove (or cornice) around the perimeter of the ceiling. (This is a job you can do yourself.) In the case of older lath and plaster ceilings, cracks tend to result from vibration or simply old age.

Cracks can also result in any kind of ceiling if the ceiling joists themselves are inadequate to support the weight of the ceiling, or if additional weights are put on the joists above, as happens when roof spaces are used for excessive storage. Where a crack in a ceiling is more than, say, 2 mm wide, and especially where the plaster on each side of the crack is not level, a more serious problem may have occurred in the structure of the building, and professional advice should be obtained.

Small 'craters', or raised dots, at regular intervals in the surface usually indicate a plasterboard ceiling where the fixing nails have either been hammered in too far or have not been hammered in far enough. The surface defects in this case can be easily repaired and then decorated.

CEILINGS

WHAT TO LOOK OUT FOR

CEILINGS

▶ **Symptom**
Cracks in the ceiling.

▶ **Cause**
a If the cracks are irregular in shape, it is probably a lath and plaster ceiling where timber laths have become loose or where plaster has lost its 'key' with the timber laths – here areas of plaster are likely to be loose. The same could apply if the plaster has been applied to concrete, which is quite likely to be the case if you live in a building designed as flats.
b If cracks are along straight lines, the ceiling is most likely to be of plasterboard panels with the cracks occurring between adjacent panels.

▶ **Remedy**
a Check the area for loose plaster – with a broom handle, for example. Do this carefully because loose areas (or even the whole ceiling) may fall down. If the problem area is fairly small, cut out the loose part, remove the laths within that area, nail plasterboard to the joists and replaster to get the repaired area flush with the remainder. Alternatively, timber battens and/ or plasterboard panels can be fixed underneath the whole ceiling area, leaving the original ceiling in place. In this case, you must make sure the additional plasterboard panels and/or battens are securely fixed *through* the original ceiling to the joists behind. If in doubt, take down the whole ceiling and replace it with plasterboard.
b Cracking between plasterboard panels does not necessarily mean there is a serious problem. Joints may be raked out and filled, using a paper or fabric covering strip across the joint before applying the

C E I L I N G S

filler. Consider lining the ceiling with a heavy lining paper to conceal the joints.

Internal Walls

Get to know the walls inside your home

Nearly all external walls are faced on the inside with either plaster (direct onto masonry), plasterboard, or some kind of panelling. In very old, good-quality houses with solid external walls, it was common practice to form an internal lining of lath and plaster, similar to that used on ceilings, or wood panelling fixed to timber uprights. This provided a degree of insulation and also kept the inside face of the wall reasonably free from penetrating damp. One of the main problems with this kind of construction, of course, was that if dampness did manage to penetrate the outer (masonry) part of the wall and come into contact with the timber, it frequently led to wet rot or dry rot in the concealed space and considerable damage occurred before the problem became visible. This continues to be a problem in properties of this type, and special vigilance is imperative in such cases.

Where outside walls are plastered directly onto masonry on the inside, the problems of dampness are, on the whole, more easily seen, enabling remedial action to be taken more quickly.

Internal walls, dividing one room from another, can be of solid or lightweight construction. In either case they can be load-bearing or non-load-bearing; and you must not assume that a wall is not load-bearing just because it sounds hollow. A large percentage of houses built 100 years or so ago, with solid outside walls, had internal load-bearing walls constructed of a timber framework faced on both sides with lath and plaster. In modern houses, timber-framed (studwork) internal walls are faced on both sides with plasterboard. These surfaces

INTERNAL WALLS

are identical to those for ceilings referred to on page 62.

Where cost or speed of construction has been an important factor, house builders have in recent years used quite thin prefabricated panels for internal walls.

A point to watch with these types of lightweight wall is that when you want to fix something heavy, like bookshelves, you should make sure you fix them to the timber uprights and not to the plaster or plasterboard in between. By tapping the wall, and listening for either a hollow or dense sound, you should be able to locate the timber uprights. Thin prefabricated panel walls do not have timber uprights and you will experience some difficulty if you want to fix anything heavy to them.

Vertical cracking often occurs at the junction between an internal lightweight wall and a solid external wall. This might be due to initial drying out (shrinkage), or could result from an inadequate fixing between the two forms of construction. If the cracking in such a location is excessive (say, more than 3 or 4 mm wide), or if the width of the crack varies throughout its height, it is possible that the outside wall has bulged, perhaps because of a lack of lateral restraint, and professional advice should be obtained before simply filling in the cracks.

If you have occasion to make holes in the walls then, with either solid or hollow construction, you must exercise special care not to interfere with electrical or plumbing services. A hand-held metal detector, with a facility for locating live electrical cables, can be purchased for a few pounds and could save you the much greater expense that would be incurred by piercing hidden cables and pipes.

Door openings tend to be the weak spots in internal walls; cracking in the wall finish above door openings, especially if the door lining itself is out of square, can indicate a structural problem and professional advice should be obtained.

Similarly, before forming a new door opening in an internal wall, or if you are thinking about removing an internal wall, you should first obtain professional advice on whether some form of alternative support, such as a steel beam, should be provided.

WHAT TO LOOK OUT FOR
INTERNAL WALLS

▶ **Symptom**
Apparent dampness on the inside of external walls.

▶ **Cause**
a Penetrating damp, which could be caused by roof leaks, defects in gutters or downpipes, porous solid walls, the 'bridging' of the cavity in cavity-built walls or design faults which encourage water to come through the wall.
b Rising damp, which could be caused by the 'bridging' of the damp-proof course, a defective damp-proof course, or no damp-proof course.
c There could be leaks in internal water services or waste pipes.
d Condensation.

▶ **Remedy**
a–c You must put a stop to the way in which water is entering the building; otherwise timber may rot and decorations will be spoiled.
d This is not so much a defect in the building, but more likely a result of the way in which the building is used. (See page 55 for further details.)

Note: Rising dampness and leaks in water services and waste pipes can also affect internal walls.

▶ **Symptom**
Cracks in the wall plaster.

INTERNAL WALLS

INTERNAL WALLS

▶ **Cause**
a Shrinkage or drying-out (in new walls or plaster).
b Differential movement, where dissimilar materials in the wall construction have expanded or contracted at different rates – such as where lintels are built over window or door openings.
c Loose plaster resulting from poor adhesion to masonry, timber laths becoming loose, or vibration.
d Structural movement, where the crack is more than, say, 2 mm wide, and especially if the plaster on each side of the crack is not level.

▶ **Remedy**
a–b Rake out the crack and apply filler. Consider fixing a cover strip (e.g., a timber batten) if the differential movement is substantial. Obtain professional advice if the vertical cracking at the junction of walls is acute.
c Carefully remove the loose plaster, refix the timber laths if insecure or replace with plasterboard and replaster.
d Obtain professional advice.

Stairs

Get to know your stairs
The construction of a timber staircase is a complicated exercise in joinery – the individual components being 'housed' (connected) into each other, to fit tightly and securely. You should not, therefore, attempt to alter or interfere with the basic structure of a staircase unless you are an experienced woodworker. While you yourself may be able to refix any loose blocks and wedges under the treads, a local joiner will almost certainly do a better and longer-lasting job. *See Figure 13.*

Stair design is strictly controlled by the Building Regu-

View underneath stairs   *Figure 13*

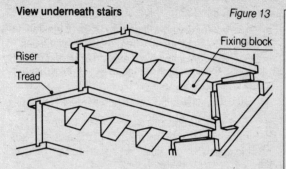

lations and, while those in an old house may not comply with current Regulations, you should not alter perfectly good stairs so that they no longer conform. The Regulations are there for your own safety, and for the safety of others who may, in the future, have to contend with your staircase. Under the current Building Regulations, these are a few of the rules which apply to staircases in private houses, where the total height of the staircase is more than 600 mm (23½ in.):

Unless leading only to a single bedroom, bathroom or lavatory, the staircase must have a clear width of 800 mm (31½ in.).

The stairs must not be steeper than 42 degrees.

There must be clear headroom of at least 2 m (6½ ft) above every part of the stairs and associated landings.

There must be a handrail 'to give firm support' on at least one side of the stairs; the handrail should be between 840 mm (33 in.) and 1 m (39 in.) above the treads.

There must be an unobstructed landing (or space) at the top and bottom of the stairs, the width and depth of the landing being at least as wide as the stairs themselves. In other words, you cannot have a doorway directly adjoining the stairs.

Where there is a drop of more than 600 mm (23½ in.) at the side, there must be a balustrade (e.g., railings) at

STAIRS

least 840 mm (33 in.) high at the side of stairs and at least 900 mm (35½ in.) high at the side of the landing. The balustrade, or railings, referred to above must be of such design that a ball of 100 mm (4 in.) diameter cannot pass through any opening. The same applies to open tread staircases; any openings must be of such a size that a 100-mm-diameter ball will not pass through.

This is not a comprehensive list of the Regulations. There are further rules governing the size of the actual treads, and stricter Building Regulations apply to common stairways – in flats, for example.

● Do your stairs comply with the rules?
● Are they safe?

WHAT TO LOOK OUT FOR

STAIRS

▶ **Symptom**
a Squeaks and creaks.
b Movement in the staircase. A loose newel post.
c A gap between the staircase string and the wall.

▶ **Cause**
a (i) Loose fixing blocks under treads.
(ii) Loose wedges where the treads are built into the string.
b (i) Inadequate support to the staircase.
(ii) Rot or woodworm infestation.
(iii) The joints between the staircase components may have opened.
c (i) The string may be inadequately fixed to the wall.
(ii) The wall may have bulged.
(iii) The wall may be damp.

▶ Remedy

a Securely refix any loose fixing blocks (with glue).

b (i) Check how the staircase is supported, i.e., how the string(s) are fixed to the wall(s); how the top of the stairs is supported; and, especially, how any tapered treads are supported. Refix these with timber packing pieces if necessary.

(ii) Check for rot, especially at the base of the newel post at ground-floor level. Check for woodworm infestation (underneath the stairs). Consider timber treatment and/or cut out and renew the affected timber if the problem is acute.

(iii) Check the joints between the components, especially where the strings are fixed to the newel post. Repair any defective joints and renew the timber dowel fixings if appropriate.

c (i) Check whether the string(s) are securely fixed to the wall(s). Refix these with plugs and screws, or expanding masonry bolts, as necessary.

(ii) Check the surface of the wall (internally and externally). Obtain professional advice if the wall has bulged and/or if a structural problem is suspected.

(iii) Check whether the wall is damp where the staircase is fixed, and cure the damp problem if necessary.

Chimney Breasts

Get to know your chimney breasts

Chimney breasts within your home are there to enclose the flues from fireplaces or boilers. In properties more than about 20 years old each flue would have been

CHIMNEY BREASTS

formed simply by building the brickwork of the chimney with a hole in the middle. The inside of that hole (the flue) would almost certainly have been lined with cement mortar. This type of construction did not always remain airtight, however, and in recent decades chimney flues have been constructed with clay-pipe linings, or built of specially shaped concrete blocks. It would be very unusual, although not unknown, for two or more flues within the same chimney to be interconnected. In older properties, however, the thin wall of brickwork between adjacent flues sometimes deteriorates, enabling smoke from one flue to enter another. Because of this possibility, it is common practice to fit a flexible metal lining when connecting a new gas fire or boiler to a flue in an old chimney.

Before blocking up old fireplaces or flues
Redundant flues should always be properly ventilated, both at the top and the bottom of the flue, so as to maintain a constant supply of fresh air within the flue itself and thus avoid stagnant, or moist, air being trapped within the structure. At the base of the flue (where the fireplace or boiler was at one time in use) an airbrick should be built in and this should be of the type that is permanently open. At the top of the flue, the chimney pot should be capped off and ventilated by means of a special terracotta fitting (available from builders' merchants) which stops rain getting in, yet, by means of a series of ventilation holes around the edge, permits air to pass through.

As an alternative, and if a redundant chimney is reduced in height, the top of the chimney may be capped off level by the use of something like a concrete paving slab bedded on cement mortar – provided that air bricks are first built into the sides of the brickwork to ventilate the flue(s) inside the closed stack.

Where the redundant flue is to be sealed at top and bottom, with ventilation provided at both levels, you must first sweep the flue to avoid the possibility of soot and dirt falling down and either blocking the low-level ventilator or coming through this ventilator into the room.

Dampness on chimney breasts

Dampness found on the face of a chimney breast, or near the top of a chimney breast below roof level, can sometimes be attributed to water penetration allowed by faulty brickwork in the chimney stack above roof level, or by an ineffective seal between the chimney and the roof covering (such as a defective lead flashing, or cracked cement fillets), where moisture has entered the structure and manifested itself internally. In this case, the problem can be cured by repointing the brickwork of the stack, by rebuilding parts of the brickwork if necessary, or by providing an effective lead flashing which makes a weathertight joint between the chimney stack and the roof covering. (See also page 18–19.)

A different kind of dampness can also occur on chimney breasts and in areas adjoining chimneys, particularly where flues are no longer used. This problem is quite common in older properties and tends to occur where a flue has been, or is still being, used by a solid fuel boiler or grate. The 'dampness' in this case results from salts within the flue migrating to the chimney-breast surface of the room.

Gases within the flue combine with moisture (especially where the structure is cool, near roof level) to form acids which react with the brickwork mortar, and, over a period, chemical salts accumulate on the surface of the plaster. When the atmosphere is humid, these salts liquefy and give the appearance of dampness, but when the atmosphere is dry this 'dampness' usually disappears. This particular problem need not necessarily be related to the moisture-penetration problem mentioned above.

When plaster has been contaminated by salts in this way the only proper remedy is to remove all of the affected plaster, thoroughly wash down the exposed brickwork (which is likely to contain further salts), treat the brickwork with a sealer and replaster using a sand and cement backing coat and Sirapite finish. (Avoid the use of lightweight plaster, such as Carlite, which does not withstand damp conditions.) This is the same remedy as that for dealing with plaster affected by rising dampness.

Taking out chimney breasts
The weight of a chimney breast, and the chimney above roof level, is considerable, especially in a building of two storeys or more. A chimney connected to an adjacent wall is still self-supporting, and you should not assume that, if you demolish part of a chimney inside the building, the remaining parts at higher level will be supported by the adjacent wall. If you want to demolish part of a chimney, or a chimney breast, you should first seek professional advice on how the remaining section(s) can be properly and safely supported.

Floors

Get to know your floors
Floors at the lowest (ground floor) level are of solid, or what is known as 'suspended timber', construction. Upper floors in houses are nearly always of timber construction, but in buildings constructed as flats, floors are normally built of concrete to achieve effective fire protection between separate flats.

A solid floor at ground level is normally constructed of concrete with a damp-proof membrane incorporated about 50 mm below the floor surface (*see Figure 14*). The purpose of the membrane is to prevent dampness from the ground reaching the surface and, if the building has been constructed properly, the membrane will join up with the damp-proof course in the walls. Damp-proof membranes have traditionally been formed of bitumen, or a similar compound, but polythene sheeting is sometimes used instead.

A defect in either the damp-proof membrane, or at the junction between the membrane and the damp-proof course in the walls, will allow moisture to enter the build-

Typical solid floor   *Figure 14*

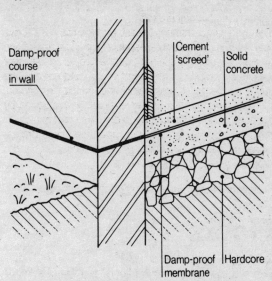

Damp-proof course in wall

Cement 'screed'

Solid concrete

Damp-proof membrane

Hardcore

FLOORS

ing in the form of rising damp, and, for this reason, you need to take care not to disturb or puncture the damp-proof membrane when carrying out any alterations or repairs around your home.

In buildings more than about 30 years old, it was common practice to finish solid floors with hard plastic tiles or wood blocks which relied solely on their fixing adhesive as the damp-proof membrane. Extra care must be taken if disturbing, or fixing things to, floors of this type, especially if the wood blocks or boards are not made of a durable hardwood. If you puncture the damp-proof membrane you could allow moisture to get up into the floor surfacing. If screwing something to a floor of this type, use a plastic plug in every screw-hole in the floor.

Suspended timber floors at ground level are built with timber boards, or wood chipboard panels, fixed to timber joists which, in turn, are supported on what are called

FLOORS

sleeper brick walls. The sleeper walls incorporate a damp-proof course, which should keep the timber components completely dry. The space under a suspended floor, which might be anything from 300 mm (12 in.) to 1 or 2 m (3–6½ ft) high, must be kept well ventilated to prevent moist air accumulating. Otherwise wet rot or dry rot could occur. Ventilation is normally provided by means of air bricks or metal ventilators built into the outside walls, and there should be a sufficient number of these on all sides of the building to maintain a good cross-flow of air under the floor at all times. It is essential to keep these ventilation openings completely clear, as mentioned on page 46 (*see Figure 15*).

Suspended timber floor   Figure 15

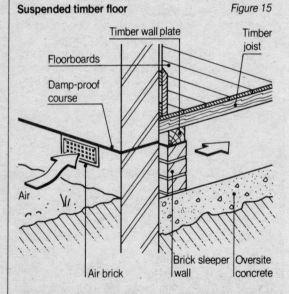

Sleeper walls supporting the floor joists must not restrict the flow of air under the floor and, for this reason, they are normally built of honeycomb brickwork, in which the bricks are spaced apart with no mortar in the vertical joints. Obviously, it is not as easy to check the condition of sleeper walls, but they are less likely to become blocked than air bricks placed around the perimeter of the building.

In modern properties, floors at ground-floor level, which may seem to be of suspended timber construction, are frequently of wood chipboard on concrete with an insulating layer of expanded polystyrene in between. Conversely, where the subsoil is not entirely suitable for supporting a conventional solid floor, an apparently solid ground floor in some modern properties could be of suspended concrete beams.

Problems with floors

Most problems with floors at ground-floor level arise from dampness of various kinds and, where timber is incorporated, there is always the risk of deterioration of the timber.

A problem which occurs in solid ground floors, especially where the floor has been levelled up on a sloping site, is that the hardcore base underneath the concrete can compact, with the result that the floor actually sinks or drops out of level. This tends to happen around the edges, or in the corners, of rooms and is frequently quite noticeable at door openings, where there is then a slight 'hump', because the wall has a sound foundation and the floor does not. A less common problem can arise in solid ground floors as a result of a chemical reaction between the concrete and certain types of hardcore material; in this case, the concrete floor expands and pushes upwards, with cracks and a 'hump' in the middle of the floor.

Upper floors are normally less likely to suffer from problems, but, if you need to refix loose floorboards, or if you need to fix anything to the floor, do be sure not to interfere with plumbing or electrical cables, which are invariably concealed just below floor level. A hand-held metal/cable detector is a useful gadget in these circumstances.

FLOORS

FLOORS

WHAT TO LOOK OUT FOR

TIMBER GROUND FLOORS

▶ **Symptom**
a Rot in the surface of the floor.
b Excessive movement.
c Individual boards or panels becoming loose.

▶ **Cause**
a This could be caused by a defective or non-existent damp-proof course; timber floors coming in contact with a damp wall; leaks in water or waste pipes; or an impervious surface (like linoleum) under which condensation has been trapped.
b There could be rotten wall plates or joists; settlement in the sleeper walls or in the 'oversite' concrete; or the joists could have deflected because of their excessive length, or by too much weight being placed on them.
c The ends of boards or panels could be inadequately supported or not properly fixed to the joists.

▶ **Remedy**
a–b Check to ensure there are no plumbing or waste-pipe leaks. Check the condition of the joists and wall plates. Check the condition of the damp-proof course. Check for a flow of fresh air under the floor. Check for evidence of wet or dry rot. Check the condition of the sleeper walls and the oversite. Seek professional advice or call in a timber preservation specialist if you are in any doubt about the soundness of the timbers or damp-proof course.
c Check to see whether the ends of any boards or panels are not being supported by a joist underneath. Securely nail or screw an additional length of timber to the side of such a joist to support

the end of the floorboard or panel. Boards and panels should be securely fixed to every joist; if there is movement between the fixing nails and the timber, consider using screws instead of nails.

SOLID GROUND FLOORS

▶ **Symptom**
a Dampness – including rot in the timber surface of a solid floor.
b Sinking or cracking.

▶ **Cause**
a There could be a defective or non-existent damp-proof membrane; or leaks in plumbing laid within the floor structure.
b There could be compaction or settlement of the hardcore underneath the concrete.

▶ **Remedy**
a Check for defective plumbing embedded in the floor (this may mean breaking out sections of the floor to expose the pipes) and repair if necessary. Check whether a damp-proof membrane exists. You must provide an effective damp-proof membrane if there is not one already.
b If the area in question, and the extent of settlement, are not excessive, it may be possible to add a levelling screed on top of the existing concrete. Otherwise you may need to break out the existing concrete and renew it. If the problem is acute, concrete can be pumped, under pressure, into gaps which have occurred under the floor.

UPPER FLOORS – TIMBER

▶ **Symptom**
a Rot in the surface of the floor.

FLOORS

79

FLOORS

b Creaking or squeaking of the floorboards or panels.
c 'Humping' of the floor surface.
d Excessive deflection.
e The floor is out of level in a bay window.

▶ **Cause**
a Leaks in the water or waste pipes.
b Inadequate fixing of the floorboards or panels.
c There is a steel beam within the floor structure and the joists have settled slightly on each side.
d The joists are of excessive length, or inadequate size, or are not braced apart adequately. Joists may have been weakened by holes being cut in them for pipes or cables to pass through.
e The structure of the bay may be inadequate (possibly following the renewal of windows).

▶ **Remedy**
a Check to ensure there are no plumbing or waste-pipe leaks.
b Secure the boards or panels to every joist. If there is movement between the fixing nails and the timber, consider using screws instead of nails.
c This is not normally a serious problem. Little can be done without lifting all the boards and 'packing up' the joists to make them level with the top of the steel beam(s).
d Provide timber struts (or 'noggins') between all joists at mid-span, if none exist already; or build in additional joists, or bolt strengthening timbers to existing joists.
e Obtain professional advice if the basic structure appears to be affected.

Services

Water and Waste

Get to know your plumbing

Water is brought into most properties by means of a water main below ground level in the road outside. Where the pipe connects to your own house, there should be a stopcock near the point of entry into your property – either in the road or footpath outside, or just inside your front garden. In older properties, terraced houses in particular, there was often a shared service, with one stopcock on the main outside and a single pipe connected to several properties in turn.

Underground water pipes should be at least 800 mm (31½ in.) below ground level to avoid the risk of frost damage. In older properties, the incoming pipe was usually made of iron or lead. Iron corrodes easily and can develop a build-up of rust inside, thus restricting the flow of water, while water can be contaminated by lead pipes – especially in soft-water areas. For these reasons, incoming water pipes to modern buildings are invariably of heavy-duty polythene.

There should be a stopcock just inside your house, where the mains water pipe enters and, ideally, there should be a drain-cock directly above, to enable all of the pipework to be drained down should it be necessary to carry out plumbing repairs.

Very often, the main stopcock is under the kitchen sink. But whether here, in the garage, or in an outside store,

WATER & WASTE

you should make quite sure you know where it is. You should also make a point of finding out the position of the outside stopcock – in case of an emergency. If the mains water pipe enters your house in a place where the temperature could drop to below freezing, the pipe should be well insulated.

All properties have a connection direct to the kitchen sink cold tap, for drinking water, but there should also be a supply to a water storage cistern at high level – probably in the main roof space. The incoming water supply will be under pressure, but water from the storage cistern to other outlets within the house flows by gravity and it is these connections which are referred to as low-pressure supplies. The pressure of water at these outlets is governed by the head (or height) of the storage cistern above the outlets.

The purpose of the water storage cistern is to keep a reasonable quantity of water available for use (not for drinking water, but for flushing toilets and for washing) should the mains supply get cut off for any reason. In older properties, and in some flats, particularly where there is insufficient 'head' (i.e., height), you might find that all pipework is fed direct from the mains supply with no provision for water storage. However, a small house should have a cistern with a capacity of at least 230 l (50 gal), and larger households should have more.

The entry of the mains-supply water into the cistern is controlled by a ball valve. A float (usually a copper or plastic ball) is fixed at the end of a projecting arm connected to the valve, and this mechanism opens or closes the valve depending on the level of water in the cistern. When the cistern is nearly full, the valve should automatically cut off. The same principle applies to toilet cisterns. Every cistern should have an overflow pipe connected at high level, and discharging outside the house, to cater for any malfunction of the ball valve; it is essential for the overflow pipe to be in a conspicuous position, of course, to give warning of any such problems (*see Figure 16*).

Where the plumbing incorporates a cold-water

WATER & WASTE

Cistern   *Figure 16*

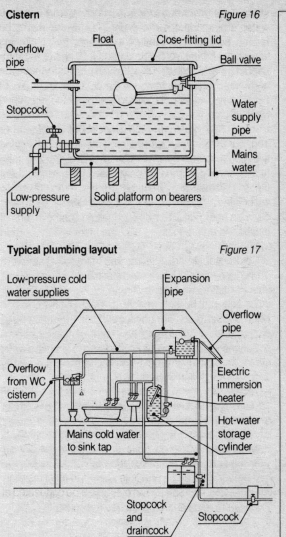

Typical plumbing layout   *Figure 17*

WATER & WASTE

storage cistern, hot water is normally stored in a hot-water storage tank or cylinder. The water might be heated by a central heating system or by an electric immersion heater. As the hot tank is fully enclosed, there should be an expansion pipe, which comes from the top of the tank to terminate above the cold-water cistern, to permit any excess hot water to overflow (*see Figure 17, page 83*).

In an older house, the pipework might be of lead or iron, but these materials present problems of corrosion and contamination, as mentioned above. Copper tube has become the most widely used material in recent times, because it overcomes a number of difficulties associated with the alternatives. Stainless steel tubing also has been used from time to time and certain kinds of plastic tubing are likely to become more widely used in the future.

Cold-water storage cisterns and hot-water tanks were at one time made of galvanised steel. But steel is susceptible to rusting, and the coating of zinc (used to protect the steel) can be susceptible to electrolytic corrosion when copper pipes are connected to it. For these reasons, cold-water cisterns are now made of rigid glass fibre or polythene, and hot-water cylinders are almost always made of copper. If your cold-water cistern is of steel, have a look inside; if there are signs of rust, arrange to have it replaced with a heavy-duty polythene cistern.

Make sure the cistern is properly supported on a sheet of exterior quality plywod over timber bearers – to spread the weight across several joists, not just two or three.

Water storage cisterns must be covered, to prevent dirt and debris from getting into the water. If located in the roof space, the cistern and associated pipework should be well insulated. The hot-water cylinder should also be insulated to conserve heat and save on fuel bills.

WHAT TO LOOK OUT FOR

WATER SUPPLY & PLUMBING

▶ **Symptom**

a Poor water pressure at the kitchen sink cold tap.

b Poor water pressure at the first-floor taps and/or shower.

c The ball valve will not shut off, causing the overflow pipe to drip.

d A dripping tap.

e A knocking noise in cold pipes.

▶ **Cause**

a (i) The incoming supply pipe may be corroded.

(ii) The incoming water supply may be shared with other properties which are drawing on it at the same times as you.

b There may be an insufficient head of water.

c (i) There may be grit in the ball valve.

(ii) There may be a defective washer, or diaphragm, in the ball valve.

(iii) There may be a defective float (a copper float might be corroded).

d A faulty or worn washer.

e This could be 'water hammer', resulting from high pressure.

▶ **Remedy**

a (i) Have the incoming supply pipe renewed.

(ii) Have a new (individual) service installed.

b Raise the level of the storage cistern. Where insufficient head cannot be achieved above a shower (usually 1 m/39 in. is needed), fit a pump to boost the water pressure to the shower.

c Clean out the ball valve. Renew the washer. Check the float and renew it if necessary. Fit a new valve

WATER & WASTE

and float assembly (they are not expensive), but make sure you use the correct type – i.e., for a high- or low-pressure supply, as appropriate.

d Renew the washer. (Some Water Authorities may do this for you free of charge – others make a nominal charge.)

e Fit a larger float (of at least 150 mm/6 in. diameter) in the cistern(s) and/or fit a float which has fins below the water level, to reduce the amount of vibration.

Get to know your waste pipes

They're not exactly a riveting conversation piece, but no home would function without them, so it's worth getting to know what happens when you pull out the plug.

Waste pipes are those pipes which get rid of waste water from sinks, baths and basins; in fact from all water-consuming fittings except water closets, or toilets. (Technically, the pipes from toilets are referred to as soil pipes, discharging soil water.)

A fitting at ground-floor level is likely to have a waste pipe discharging to a gulley outside, with the pipe terminating either above, or below, a grating. Gratings do prevent any solid matter from possibly clogging up the drains, but they can, nevertheless, get into an unhygienic condition if not cleaned out on a regular basis. They can easily become blocked by leaves, for example, unless you fit a chicken-wire grid, or make a wooden lid to fit across the top of the kerb which is normally built around the grating. In recent years, however, back-inlet gullies have become commonplace – mainly as a result of a Building Regulations requirement for waste water not to be discharged in mid-air, i.e., above a grating. Waste-water gullies normally have a built-in water trap to enable any accumulation of solid matter (such as potato peelings, for example) to be removed from the gulley itself instead of going down the drain.

Until a few years ago, waste pipes from fittings not at ground-floor level were often designed to discharge into

WATER & WASTE

a hopper. But as the hopper was invariably situated some height above ground level, it could become blocked (again from leaves, for example) and waste water could then overflow – resulting in an unhygienic state of affairs, not to mention the saturation of the wall to which the hopper was fixed.

Mainly as a result of a Building Regulations requirement, waste pipes from fittings above ground-floor level are now normally connected physically – either to a soil pipe or to a vertical waste pipe (like a soil pipe, but sometimes of a smaller diameter).

If your waste pipes discharge into a hopper which tends to get blocked with leaves, you could think about fitting chicken wire across the top of the hopper, or investigate the possibility of rerouting the waste pipes to connect directly to a soil pipe.

In older properties, waste pipes were nearly always made of lead. Steel and copper have been used in more recent times, but plastic pipes and fittings have been adopted almost exclusively nowadays. The cost of plastic, compared with the alternatives, has been the main reason for this, but the well-engineered design of modern waste traps and other components could be said to be an improvement on the earlier, metal fittings. Plastic waste pipes are almost trouble-free, provided they are adequately supported to cope with their slightly flexible nature.

HAVE YOU GOT SMELLY PIPES?

▶ **Symptoms**
Smells, or strange gurgling noises, coming out of the plughole of your bath, basin or sink, or out of the waste pipe to which your washing machine connects.

▶ **Cause**
Perhaps there is no trap (or U-bend) in the waste-

WATER & WASTE

WATER & WASTE

water pipe, or, if there is, the small volume of water which should remain in the trap (i.e., the water seal) is probably getting sucked out by a vacuum further down the pipe. If the waste pipe is very long and of too small a diameter, the sheer volume of, say, a bathful of water being released all at once will create a vacuum. And if a bath and basin (or more waste fittings) all connect to the same pipe, the volume of water being released from one of the fittings can affect the water seal in the traps of the others. The problem can be acute in buildings divided into flats if there are a number of baths, basins, etc., all connected to the same waste pipe.

▶ Remedy

First of all you need to check that there is, in fact, a waste trap close to the fitting itself. Usually, the trap is connected directly to the waste outlet (i.e., underneath the basin, etc.). Waste pipes which have been provided for washing machines frequently have no trap at all, so the simple answer is to fit one.

If a trap is fitted, but is not working effectively, you need to overcome the problem caused by a vacuum in the waste pipe. Replacing small-diameter pipes with larger ones, or connecting special ventilating pipes, might be difficult – and in any case this is likely to be expensive. A simpler remedy is to replace the trap itself.

A trap with a 25-mm (1 in.) deep seal, for example, can be replaced with one having a 75-mm (3 in.) deep seal (the larger volume of water will be more likely to remain in the trap). A 75-mm (3 in.) deep seal 'bottle' trap is bulkier than other types, but has the advantage of instant access for cleaning purposes. You can also get a special kind of bottle trap which is fitted with a one-way air inlet valve, which will let air in to prevent a vacuum occurring yet will remain sealed to stop smells getting out. This is usually the most convenient way of getting over the problem.

Different types of waste trap

Figure 18

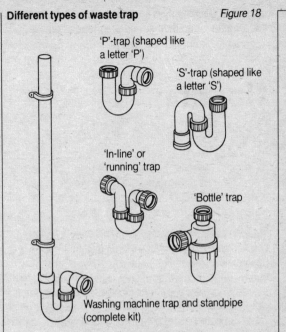

'P'-trap (shaped like a letter 'P')

'S'-trap (shaped like a letter 'S')

'In-line' or 'running' trap

'Bottle' trap

Washing machine trap and standpipe (complete kit)

If, for some reason, you cannot, or do not want to, fit a trap directly underneath the basin, you can fit what is called an in-line trap, or make up a trap using standard bends or other components from the very wide range of plastic pipe fittings currently on the market. The push-fit system of jointing plastic pipes makes it very easy to achieve watertight joints.

Do be sure to use the correct size of pipes and fittings: 32 mm (1¼ in.) diameter for single basins and bidets, but 38 mm (1½ in.) diameter for baths, showers and sinks. Do make sure that waste pipes slope in the right direction (water will not run uphill!) and be sure to support the pipes so that they do not sag; plastic clips to suit the size of pipe are needed, not more than, say, 900 mm (36 in.) apart.

Most plastic waste traps cost only a few pounds

HEATING

each, and are usually not too difficult to fit, especially if the waste pipes themselves are made of plastic.

Heating

Get to know your heating system

The main component in any kind of heater is a heat exchanger. Even a kettle of water on an open fire is a heat exchanger, with the heat of the fire being transferred to the water. The enormous variety of heaters available all work on this simple heat exchange principle, whether for water heating or for space (room) heating.

Independent water heaters (with no means of storage)

Old-fashioned water geysers, or gas multi-point water heaters, provide instant hot water by means of a gas burner underneath a container of water or a zig-zag of pipes. Whenever the water tap is turned on, the flow of water automatically turns on the gas supply and the water is heated as it flows through the heat exchanger. Small heaters of this type usually have a swivel spout over the bowl or basin. Multi-points are so called because they are connected by pipes to taps at two or more (multiple) outlets.

Certain types of small gas water heaters can be installed without a flue to the outside air, but they do give off large volumes of water vapour and can, therefore, cause excessive condensation unless the room is well ventilated. Multi-point water heaters should never be installed in a bathroom unless they are of the 'room-sealed' type – where air is drawn directly into the heater from outside the house and not from within the room. If you have an old type of multi-point or water heater which relies on air from within the room in which it is installed, do have it checked thoroughly (by the Gas Board or by a registered gas engineer), and be prepared to stop using it if it is an old model. It could be dangerous.

'Instantaneous' electric water heaters have become popular, principally due to their small size, and these are especially convenient where a relatively small flow of water is required – such as for a shower. The heating element in these is usually of several kilowatts' rating and this type of heater is not really economic if large volumes of hot water are required. The principle of operation is the same as for an instantaneous gas water heater; the electric heating element is automatically switched on by the flow of water through the heater.

Independent water heaters which store hot water
Gas circulators operate like the kind of small instantaneous heater you find fitted over a sink, except that they are connected to a hot-water tank or cylinder and are often used in conjunction with warm-air heating systems.

Heating a volume of water by electricity is most commonly done by a heating element immersed in a tank of water (i.e., an immersion heater). When hot water is drawn off at the taps, the tank or cylinder is replenished either by a low-pressure supply from a cold-water storage cistern or, in small units where only a small volume of water is to be heated, direct from the mains supply. There is also a special kind of unit which incorporates a compact cold-water storage cistern directly above the hot-water container, all enclosed in a single 'package'.

Water heating from boilers
There are two basic types of system, either direct or indirect, and in both types the boiler may be heated by solid fuel, oil or gas. With the direct system, water heated by the boiler is piped to the storage cylinder and it is this same water which is drawn off for use at the taps. This type of system is rarely used nowadays.

In the indirect system, water heated by the boiler is piped to a heat exchanger, often in the shape of a coil of pipework inside the storage cylinder. The same volume of water circulates through the boiler and heat exchanger but is not piped to the taps – this is called the primary circuit. A different circuit conveys water from the cold-water storage cistern to the cylinder, where it is heated by the heat exchanger and then piped to the hot taps – this is called the secondary circuit (*see Figure 19*).

Both systems require an expansion pipe to each circuit. Additionally, there should be a safety valve on the

'Indirect' heating system for hot water   *Figure 19*

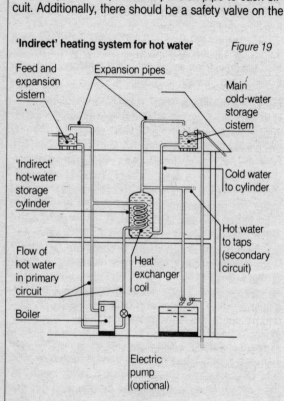

Feed and expansion cistern

Expansion pipes

Main cold-water storage cistern

'Indirect' hot-water storage cylinder

Cold water to cylinder

Flow of hot water in primary circuit

Heat exchanger coil

Hot water to taps (secondary circuit)

Boiler

Electric pump (optional)

boiler or on the primary circuit near the boiler, in case of an excessive build-up of pressure.

In hard-water areas, when water is heated to much more than about 80°C (176°F), chalky scale can form on the inside of the pipes and in the heat exchanger and storage cylinder. In the direct type of heating system,

92

where fresh water is continually drawn in, the problem of scale, or furring-up of pipes, can become acute and, for this reason, indirect systems are much more common.

Central heating using hot water
Independent of providing hot water to the taps (or sometimes in addition), a boiler run on solid fuel, oil or gas can be used for heating the rooms, i.e., as central heating. The output of heat into each room is most commonly achieved by means of radiator panels, but, alternatively, it can be by means of convectors (essentially pipes with fins on them, usually boxed in just above floor level) and sometimes by fan-assisted.convectors (where an electrically-operated fan blows the heat from the finned pipes into the room). Some boilers are known as back-boilers – that is, where they are at the back of an open (solid fuel or gas) fire.

The circulation of water in some older central heating systems relies on gravity, with warm water rising from the boiler, and cooler water returning to the boiler at the lower end of the system.

A more efficient arrangement is achieved when the water is pumped around the pipework, as is the case with all modern systems.

For a more even distribution of hot water to the radiators, a two-pipe system incorporates separate flow and return pipes, whereby the cooler water leaving each radiator is returned to the boiler via a separate circuit. Nearly all modern central heating systems which rely on hot-water circulation are of this type.

In all of these arrangements, hot water from the boiler can also be piped to a hot-water storage cylinder. The combined layout is shown in *Figure 20* (*page 94*).

Variations on the types of central heating system mentioned above include a special kind of hot-water storage cylinder which can be fed direct from the mains supply, without the need for a low-pressure supply from a cold-water storage cistern. There are also modern high-pressure systems where the boiler is fed direct from the mains

HEATING

Central heating and hot water system *Figure 20*

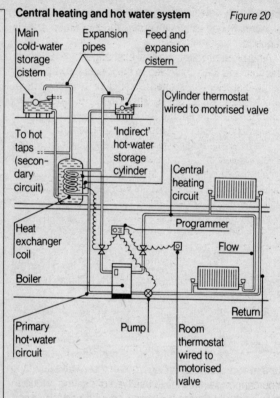

supply and is able to provide instantaneous hot water to the taps in addition to central heating; but bye-laws in some areas might not permit this kind of arrangement.

Warm-air heating
Warm-air central heating circulates air, instead of water, to heat the rooms. Heat is produced in a unit run on gas or oil, needing a flue, or on electricity, which does not require a flue. Most types of electric warm-air heating units are designed to be run on cheaper 'off-peak' electricity. They have a core of special bricks which are heated up during the night and then the heat is distributed during

the day. There is usually also an option of running the unit on normal-price electricity during the day if more heat is required.

Air is blown through the heat exchanger by a fan within the unit, and then conveyed to the rooms through ducts (large-diameter pipes, often rectangular in cross section) which end in outlet grilles. The grilles are usually fitted with dampers, to enable the supply of warm air to be stopped off if heat is not required in that particular room.

Warm-air distribution ducts may be built in below floor level, located in the roof space, or sometimes boxed in within the building. After the warm air has been distributed to the rooms, it finds its way back to the heating unit where it is sucked in, reheated, and recirculated. Normally gaps are needed under the doors, or else grilles must be fitted into the doors, to allow the recirculation of air back to the heating unit. An advantage with most units of this type is that, in the summer, the heat exchanger can be switched off and the fan run on its own to circulate cool air.

One of the main drawbacks with this kind of heating is that any unpleasant smells or cooking odours will tend to be circulated through the system to all the rooms in the building, and the system might be noisy.

Under-floor electric heating
You cannot normally have this type of heating added to an existing building, but many new homes with solid floors have had under-floor heating built in during construction. Electric heating elements, spaced close together, are incorporated in the concrete just below floor level and are heated up by means of cheaper off-peak electricity; the concrete floor itself is heated during the night and the heat is then distributed during the day. This can be an effective form of heating when operating properly. However, once the floor has been heated up, you have little control over the rate of heat output. This type of heating installation has a lifespan of about 25 years.

HEATING

Electric ceiling heating

Again, you cannot normally have this system added to an existing building, and it is less common than alternative forms of heating. Closely spaced electric heating elements are built in just above the plasterboard ceilings and infra-red heat is radiated downwards. Compared with under-floor heating, you have better control over the rate of heat output. It is essential to maintain good insulation above the heating elements to minimise wasted heat.

Electric storage radiators

Whether or not you classify these as central heating might depend on whether or not there is a central control panel to which all such radiators are wired up. They do not count as central heating as far as the rateable value of your house is concerned, because they are regarded as 'portable'. In any event, they need to have independent electric circuits, as they are not designed to be plugged in to the normal house wiring system.

Storage radiators have a core of special bricks which are heated up during the night by means of cheaper off-peak electricity. The heat is then dissipated by the hot bricks during the day. Some storage radiators also incorporate a fan, to blow heat into the room. There is not normally an option of also running storage radiators on normal-price electricity.

The advantages of this type of space heating are that the installation cost is usually low, and you can, if you wish, add more heaters to an existing system quite easily. The main disadvantages are that the radiators themselves tend to be bulky (necessary to accommodate the volume of bricks inside), and you cannot control the heat output as easily as with other forms of heating. Once the bricks have been heated up, you cannot afterwards decide that you do not want them 'on'. Moreover, the electric elements inside become brittle after a few years and are likely to break if you then move the radiators. Electric storage radiators tend to be suitable for steady background heating.

Independent heaters

Individual room heaters can be fixed to the wall or be portable, and are run on electricity, gas or paraffin. Gas (especially bottled gas) and paraffin heaters give off large volumes of water vapour and will cause condensation problems unless there is adequate ventilation. There tends to be a greater risk of fire with portable heaters of any kind and their use should be avoided in houses occupied by children, or by elderly or disabled people.

Where you have a series of fixed room heaters which incorporate timeclocks and/or thermostats, there is a close resemblance to central heating.

Some kinds of fixed gas-fired room-sealed convector heaters incorporate such controls and can provide an economic form of space heating. These heaters are relatively small and need to be located on external walls as they incorporate short flues, which have to extend outside. Like electric storage radiators, you can normally add more heaters to an existing system quite easily. There is no 'central' control, however.

Boiler flues

The majority of domestic gas boilers (and most gas water heaters) are now of the room-sealed type, incorporating a balanced flue which draws in combustion air direct from the outside. This type of flue is usually a very short length of pipe, just projecting through an outside wall. Where the boiler has a conventional flue, i.e., piped to a chimney, combustion air is taken from within the room in which the boiler is installed. In this case, it is essential to have permanent ventilation to the room from the outside air, otherwise the boiler will not operate efficiently and there will be a risk of toxic fumes building up indoors. A solid fuel or oil-fired boiler must also have a permanent supply of combustion air to the room in which it is installed.

Central heating controls

Most people, when they get estimates for having central heating installed, usually pick the least expensive estimate. This is understandable when you are confronted

HEATING

HEATING

with two or three estimates which all look as though they are offering exactly the same thing. A similar situation arises when a new house is built; the builder invariably puts in the least expensive system to keep down the total cost of the house.

Heating installers usually provide a big enough boiler, and big enough radiators, to make sure you get enough heat. But all too often the cheapest control equipment is used, irrespective of whether or not it is appropriate. The result is that you get too much heat – in other words, high running costs and a waste of heat – or a poor distribution of heat, with some areas too hot and others not hot enough. More often than not, you find you are unable to control the heating and hot water at the times of day when you want them. It might well be possible, however, to adapt or augment your present control system for improved comfort and greater economy.

Because of the wide range of controls available, and because of the numerous permutations of how they can be incorporated, not to mention the variety of heating lay-outs, there is no single 'right' or 'wrong' control system. You would need to discuss with an experienced heating engineer which would be the most advantageous and the most practical in your own home, but the following may serve as a guide to the main components.

Pump
In a system which relies on hot-water circulation, an electrically operated pump moves the heated water around the pipework, instead of hot-water movement being achieved solely by convection and gravity (as happens in old-fashioned systems). The pump can be switched on and off manually, or automatically by a programmer (see page 101). The pump must be of the right size to produce the correct rate of flow. In large properties, the secondary circuit can also be pumped, to reduce the time it takes for hot water to reach the taps.

Boiler thermostat

Most boilers have a thermostat built in to regulate the temperature of the hot water leaving the boiler. The thermostat is a kind of electrical switch with a dial on the front which you can adjust yourself. When the temperature of the circulating water reaches the pre-set limit, the boiler automatically turns itself off; when the temperature of the water falls below the pre-set limit, the boiler automatically comes on again. The calculated output of radiators and convectors is based on the circulating water being at a particular temperature, normally about 70°C (160°F), and you may finish up with an uneven heat output from the radiators or convectors if you set the boiler thermostat too low. There may be some merit in adjusting the boiler thermostat to the lowest setting if you especially want a low heat output, while the house is unoccupied, for example. As a precaution against freezing up in very cold weather, however, a better solution would be to rely on a frost-stat (see page 100).

Room thermostat

An adjustable thermostat fitted to the wall in one of the rooms (usually the main living-room), or in the entrance hall, will 'sense' the air temperature in the location where it is installed. If that air temperature is below the pre-set level, the thermostat will switch the heating system on. When the air temperature reaches the required level, the thermostat will automatically switch the heating system off. Depending on the type of heating system and the type of boiler, a room thermostat may be wired up to control the boiler itself, or the circulating pump, or to open or close a motorised (electrically operated) valve in the pipework.

A room thermostat should be positioned approximately 1.5 m (4 ft 9 ins.) above floor level; much lower and the heat output will tend to be higher, much higher and the heat output will tend to be lower.

As even a 1°C reduction in temperature can reduce your heating bill by as much as 8 per cent, it pays to make

HEATING

HEATING

sure the thermostat is working efficiently. A new room thermostat is an inexpensive item, so it could be worth renewing your existing one if it is more than a few years old.

The main drawback to relying on a single room thermostat for the principal means of control is that, if the place where the thermostat is located suddenly becomes cold, the heating system will start to run, and other parts of the house may become too hot. Conversely, if the place where the thermostat is located suddenly becomes warm, the heating system will stop running, and other parts of the house may become too cold. Two (or more) room thermostats could be used to control different zones, however (see page 102).

Frost-stat
A kind of room thermostat, but with a dial showing very low temperatures, a frost-stat can be connected up and set to switch the heating system on when the temperature falls below a pre-set level.

If the boiler for your central heating system is located in an outbuilding or some other unheated area, you should think about installing a frost-stat to minimise the risk of freezing up in very cold weather.

Thermostatic radiator valves
These non-electric valves can be fitted to individual radiators and are almost certainly the single most cost-effective way of reducing excessive heat, and thereby reducing your heating costs. A TRV (thermostatic radiator valve) cannot get *more* heat out of a radiator, only *less*. It will not provide an answer for a radiator that is already too small for the size of the room, but what it will do is to reduce the heat output from a radiator automatically when the room reaches the temperature you want. Unlike a room thermostat, designed to control heat output throughout the entire house, individual TRVs control the heat output in individual rooms. Each TRV can be set, or varied, depending on the room temperature required. If, for example, you want only a low temperature in a little-

used room, you will be able to achieve this instantly. TRVs are not especially expensive and, fitted throughout the house, could reduce heating bills by up to 20 per cent.

Three-way mixing valve

This type of valve can be manually operated or electrically controlled (by a thermostat or programmer). It is connected into the circulating-water pipework for the purpose of mixing cooler water, returning from the radiators, with hot water leaving the boiler, whenever full reheating of the circulating water is not required – for example, when the weather is mild. This enables the boiler to provide more heat for the primary circuit of the domestic hot-water pipework. In cold weather, when the boiler is running almost constantly, the domestic hot water can overheat.

Compensating system

This is a more sophisticated control system, incorporating a three-way mixing valve and designed to vary the boiler output automatically, according to a number of factors, including both indoor and outdoor temperatures. Compensating control systems cause the boiler to run more smoothly, instead of continually stopping and starting, and are said to reduce heating costs by some 10 per cent.

Timeclocks and programmers

Many heating systems rely on a single timeclock, which switches both the heating and hot water on or off at the same time – irrespective of whether or not you need both at once. This problem can be overcome by installing a programmer, which allows you to control the heating and hot water independently of each other.

Some makes of boiler have a timeclock or programmer built in. Most programmers have two separate on/off settings for each 24-hour period (with an over-ride facility, including 'continuous on' and 'continuous off' settings).

Once set, the on/off settings remain the same for each day of the week. For greater control over the heating periods, you could install a 'seven-day' programmer, which allows you to select different on/off settings for different days of the week. As an example, you could set it to switch your heating system on and off at certain times during the week and at different times at the weekend; you would not then have to remember to alter the clock controls manually for different heating periods.

It need not be a major job to change a '24-hour' programmer for a 'seven-day' version, but the task does require a good knowledge of basic electrics.

Zoning

Zoning is where you have two or more separate pipework circuits (or zones), each connected to the main boiler, yet each controlled by a separate timeclock or thermostat. A typical arrangement in a two-storey house would be to have one zone downstairs and one zone upstairs; you could then have the heating on at different times on each floor level, with a consequent saving in running costs. Alternatively (or additionally), you could have a separate zone for the circuit to the hot-water cylinder, enabling you to have water heated at different times from the central heating periods, again saving money by not having to run both the heating and domestic hot-water systems during the same time periods.

However, this is usually only an economic proposition if you are starting from scratch. Pipework alterations to an existing installation could prove quite expensive but it might, nevertheless, be worth considering if you have a large house at present all on a single zone.

Cylinder thermostat

There is no point in heating the water in your hot-water cylinder beyond the point where it is so hot that you have to add cold water to it to cool it down. To do this is an obvious waste of money. Furthermore, in hard-water areas, exceptionally hot water can cause limescale to form in the cylinder. Two basic controls will solve these problems:

1   You can have a thermostatic control valve fitted into the primary-circuit pipework returning to the boiler. This is a non-electric type of valve and is pre-set manually. It operates just like a thermostatic radiator valve, but, in this case, it stops the flow of hot water around the primary circuit when the water stored in the cylinder reaches the required temperature.

2   Alternatively, you can have a cylinder thermostat fixed to the side of the hot-water cylinder. This is like a room thermostat, but has a dial on the front which you adjust to select the temperature to which you want the cylinder water heated. It is wired up to open or close a motorised (electrically operated) valve in the pipework between the boiler and cylinder and, again, this thermostat will stop the flow of hot water around the primary circuit when the water stored in the cylinder reaches the required temperature. Modern cylinder thermostats are quite cheap; if yours looks old, or is clogged up with dust or dirt, you should think about having it renewed.

You should not restrict the flow of hot water through the cylinder if your heating system is of a type with a solid-fuel or oil-fired boiler, which relies on the cylinder to dissipate excess heat after the boiler is stopped down. Check this point with a qualified heating engineer before fitting a cylinder thermostat.

Three-way diverting valve
This is similar to the three-way mixing valve described above, but this valve causes the hot water leaving the boiler to be diverted either to the radiators, or to the cylinder, or (in a mid-way position) to both. It is usually in the form of a motorised (electrically operated) valve, automatically controlled by a room thermostat *and* cylinder thermostat, via a programmer.

A diverting valve is often found at the heart of an inexpensive control system – except where the boiler is a solid-fuel or an oil-fired type, which must not have a

HEATING

restriction in water flow through the cylinder primary circuit. Heating installations which rely on this kind of arrangement may prove incapable of providing sufficient heat for both central heating and domestic hot water at the same time, especially in very cold weather.

WHAT TO LOOK OUT FOR

HOT WATER FROM CENTRAL HEATING

▶ **Symptom**
a A poor flow of hot water.
b The tap water is too hot.
c The tap water is not hot enough.

▶ **Cause**
a (i) The cold-water storage cistern is not placed high enough to get sufficient 'head' (pressure) of water.
  (ii) There may be air trapped in the pipework.
  (iii) There is limescale in the pipework and/or cylinder (often visible around the spouts of taps).
b (i) A faulty or incorrectly adjusted cylinder thermostat.
  (ii) No cylinder thermostat.
c (i) The pipe from the cylinder to the tap is too long and/or inadequately insulated.
  (ii) There may be air trapped in the pipework.
  (iii) Limescale in the primary circuit.
  (iv) A faulty cylinder thermostat.
  (v) The boiler and/or cylinder is inefficient or not big enough.
  (vi) The feed and expansion cistern is empty, with insufficient water in the system.

▶ **Remedy**

a (i) Raise the level of the cistern or increase the size of the supply pipe.

(ii) Flush through, or fit an air release valve. Make sure the vent pipe from the top of the cylinder runs upwards to its open end above the cistern, with no downhill lengths.

(iii) Get a plumber to descale the pipework and cylinder using a chemical descaling fluid. If you have a direct cylinder, change to the indirect type.

b Adjust the cylinder thermostat or fit a new cylinder thermostat. **Note:** check with a heating engineer first.

c (i) Insulate the hot-water pipe from cylinder to tap. If the length of pipe is very long, investigate the possibility of installing a pump in the secondary circuit.

(ii) Flush through, or fit an air release valve. Make sure the vent pipe from the top of the cylinder runs upwards to its open end above the cistern, with no downhill lengths.

(iii) Get a plumber to descale the primary circuit and boiler.

(iv) Adjust the cylinder thermostat or fit a new cylinder thermostat. **Note:** check with a heating engineer first.

(v) Consult a heating engineer about the size of the boiler and/or hot-water cylinder.

(vi) Check the feed and expansion cistern and adjust or renew the ball valve if necessary.

CENTRAL HEATING – NOISES AND CORROSION

▶ **Symptom**

a Knocking noises from the pipes or boiler.

b Creaking or cracking noises from the pipework.

c Rusty-coloured water from the hot taps (especially

HEATING

after drawing off a large volume of hot water).
d Corrosion at the bottom of steel radiators, or in a galvanised steel cistern or hot-water tank.

▶ Cause

a Excessive limescale in the pipework and/or in the boiler.
b Thermal expansion/contraction of pipes in contact with the structure.
c (i) Corrosion in the cold-water storage cistern (see also (d) below).
   (ii) If a direct system, there may be corrosion in the boiler.
d (i) Scraps of metal (e.g., nails or metal filings) may have been deposited in the system at the time of installation.
   (ii) Electrolytic corrosion due to the combination of copper and galvanised steel components.

▶ Remedy

a Descale the boiler, and possibly the entire heating system; this is usually best left to a heating engineer.
b Check for pipework with insufficient space for thermal movement, such as where pipes pass through floor joists. It may be difficult to make more space for thermal movement without first disconnecting the pipe(s).
c (i) Replace a galvanised steel cistern with a glass-fibre or polythene equivalent. Galvanised steel cisterns can be cleaned and painted inside with bituminous paint, but this is seldom an economic proposition.
   (ii) If you have a direct cylinder, convert it to an indirect type.
d (i) Thoroughly clean out (flush) the entire system. This is usually best left to a heating engineer. The radiator panels may have to be renewed.
   (ii) Replace a steel hot-water tank with a copper hot-water cylinder. See also (c) (i) above.

INEFFICIENT CENTRAL HEATING

▶ **Symptom**

a No heat from the boiler.

b The radiator panels do not become hot enough, or some panels are hotter than others.

c The radiator panels get hot at the bottom but not at the top.

d The warm-air heating system is inadequate.

e In the under-floor heating system, some areas get very hot, while other areas remain cold.

▶ **Cause**

a (i) The boiler thermostat and/or programmer may be faulty.

(ii) The boiler fuel valve or thermocouple may be faulty.

b (i) This is an inherent problem in a one-pipe heating system.

(ii) The circulating pump may be faulty.

(iii) The control system(s) may be inadequate.

(iv) Air may be trapped in the pipework.

(v) Inadequate 'balancing' (i.e., adjustment of the flow valves) at the time of installation. This can be upset if the valves are shut off for servicing and later opened again.

(vi) There may be limescale in the boiler, or the boiler may be inadequate.

c Air trapped in the radiators, or insufficient water in the system.

d (i) An inefficient heater unit (too old or too small).

(ii) Inadequate control system(s).

e Some heating elements may no longer be operating.

▶ **Remedy**

a (i) Check the fuel supply to the boiler. (If gas, see

HEATING

HEATING

if the pilot light is lit.) Check the boiler thermostat.

(ii) Check the electricity supply to the boiler. Replace the fuse if necessary.

(iii) Check the timeclock/programmer. (Switch on to test it, and see if the motorised valves operate.)

(iv) Check the room thermostat. Adjust or renew this.

(v) Get a heating engineer to test the boiler and its controls.

b (i) If you have a one-pipe system, there is little that can be done without converting to a two-pipe system, but see (b) (v) below.

(ii) Check the circulating pump.

(iii) Check all controls, especially thermostats and timeclock/programmer.

(iv) Flush through, or fit an air release valve. See also (c) below.

(v) Balance all the flow valves, which control the flow of hot water through the different parts of the system and also through each radiator (the 'lockshield' valve). This is normally a tricky job and is best left to a heating engineer.

(vi) Descale the boiler, and possibly the entire heating system. This is usually best left to a heating engineer. The boiler may need to be replaced if it is more than, say, 15 years old. (Boilers with cast-iron heat exchangers usually last longer than those with pressed-steel heat exchangers.)

c (i) Release any trapped air by temporarily opening the air bleed valve at the top of each radiator panel.

(ii) Make sure the feed and expansion cistern contains water. Check the water supply and ball valve.

(iii) Check for leaks in the system. (Where water

can get out, air can also get in.) Repair any leaks.

d (i) Change the filter element. (A clogged filter will affect air circulation.)

(ii) Check the control(s) (timeclock and thermostats).

(iii) Have the heating unit serviced.

e (i) Check and replace any faulty fuses.

(ii) Usually there is little that can be done once elements embedded in a solid floor have failed. It is not really an economic proposition to dig up the floor to renew faulty elements.

Insulation

Why do we bother to insulate? The answer is simple. Insulation keeps the heat in and the cold out, and therefore makes the house more comfortable to live in. But more important than this, good insulation can reduce winter heating bills dramatically.

You may hear professionals or insulation salesmen talking about U-values and wonder what this means. The U-value of a particular form of building construction (say, a wall, window or roof) is the numerical value given to it for the amount of heat which will pass through it in a given period of time. The lower the U-value, the less heat will pass through, and hence the better the insulation it will provide. It follows that you should aim to achieve the lowest U-value possible for each part of your home.

In an uninsulated house, 25 per cent of the total heat loss is through the roof; 45 per cent is through the walls (roughly 35 per cent through the walls themselves and about 10 per cent through the windows); a further heat loss of about 15 per cent is through the ground floor; the other 15 per cent is lost through draughts, mostly around doors and windows.

INSULATION

The roof

Good roof insulation will cut the total heat loss through that part of the structure down to 10, or even 5, per cent and is easy to achieve in a pitched roof. With a few simple precautions, you can tackle this as a really worthwhile DIY job.

Insulation placed between, or across, the ceiling joists will keep heat within the rooms below and will reduce the amount of heat getting up into the roof space – where it is effectively wasted (*see Figure 21*).

Loft insulation   Figure 21

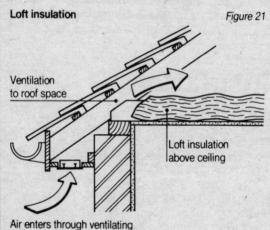

Ventilation to roof space

Loft insulation above ceiling

Air enters through ventilating holes in soffit board at eaves

You should aim for a minimum thickness of 100 mm (4 in.) or 150 mm (6 in.) if possible. If some insulation already exists you can normally leave this in place and add a further layer above. The whole of the roof area should be insulated in this way, except directly underneath any cold-water storage cisterns, where some heat should be allowed to rise to minimise the risk of freezing in very cold weather.

The materials to use are either glass fibre or mineral wool, both of which are usually sold in polythene-wrapped rolls and are available in a range of thicknesses.

Alternatively, you can use expanded polystyrene or vermiculite granules, which are normally sold in paper sacks. You simply empty these out between the ceiling joists – after fixing short lengths of boards between the ends of the ceiling joists to prevent the granules from dropping down into the eaves at the sides of the roof. To provide 100 mm (4 in.) thick insulation in the roof of a typical semi-detached house, with an area of about 40 sq m (48 sq yd), you would need around 36 sacks of the granular material or, alternatively, about 25 rolls of glass-fibre mat. On balance, the granular material is easy to deal with, but costs about twice as much as the equivalent volume of glass-fibre mat. It is always a good idea to provide the same thickness of insulation on the top side of the roof trap-door access hatch.

If you decide to install glass-fibre mat yourself, you may find that your eyes and skin are irritated by the fine fibres and you are, therefore, recommended to wear a dust mask and rubber gloves, which are not expensive and are available from builders' merchants or DIY shops.

Putting insulation, or extra insulation, in a flat roof is not so straightforward. If you put an insulation layer underneath the roof you must be quite sure to incorporate a vapour barrier (an airtight layer of something like polythene) below the level of the insulation to stop water vapour from within the house getting into the space inside the flat roof where it could condense and cause damage to the timbers.

Flat roofs can sometimes be insulated by adding a layer of insulation on top of the roof surface, but in this case you should get advice on weatherproofing, and on how to secure the insulation, from a qualified surveyor.

Caution
It is important to make sure your roof space is permanently ventilated, especially after putting in a thick layer of insulation. There is a tendency for water vapour, or moist air from within the house, to accumulate in an unventilated roof space, and this can cause damage to

INSULATION

the timbers. If the roof tiles have a layer of underfelt, making the roof space almost airtight, it is essential to provide adequate ventilation – either at the eaves or in gable end walls, and possibly at the ridge level as well. The current Building Regulations require the level of ventilation to be equivalent to a 12-mm (½ in.) wide gap running continuously around the eaves. (A number of special products for providing eave ventilation have come onto the market in recent years. They consist mostly of plastic disks or strips, fitted with wire gauze to keep out insects. You can get further details from most builders' merchants.)

You should take care to avoid allowing plastic-covered electric cables and expanded polystyrene insulation to come into contact with each other in the roof space, or elsewhere. A chemical reaction can take place between these two materials, with the result that the plastic covering on the cables becomes quite sticky. You should, in any case, avoid covering electric cables with insulation in case they overheat.

Walls

As, in most houses, the total area taken up by windows is quite small, you need to consider whether the walls themselves are sufficiently well insulated.

In older properties, solid walls give very poor insulation and conduct heat out of the building very quickly. The most economic method of insulating solid walls is to provide an inner lining, perhaps with an air cavity and/or an insulating material between the inner lining and the solid wall. This can be done, for example, by securely fixing timber battens to the inside surface of the solid wall and then nailing sheets of plasterboard to the battens. You can achieve a very satisfactory result if you use taper-edged plasterboard (commonly used in modern timber-framed houses), because the joints can be made invisible without having to plaster the whole surface. The battens must be fixed vertically, to allow air to circulate from top to bottom, and should be of timber which has been pressure-treated with preservative.

The space between the battens can be filled with glass fibre or polystyrene boards, but, in any event, you should also incorporate a polythene-sheet vapour barrier across the front of the battens, immediately behind the plasterboard, to prevent moisture from within the room getting into the space behind, where it could condense on the cold surface of the solid wall and cause damage to the structure. It is possible to buy sheets of taper-edged plasterboard which have a backing of expanded polystyrene and also incorporate a vapour barrier; details can be obtained from good builders' merchants.

Cavity-built walls provide better insulation than solid walls because they incorporate an insulating air space. Over the past 25 years or so, the building blocks for the inner leaf of cavity-built walls have generally been made of lightweight (aerated) concrete which, in itself, is a good insulating material. Some modern buildings are constructed of solid walls built entirely of these lightweight concrete blocks (faced on the outside with a coating of cement, or a weatherproof cladding), achieving much better insulation than an equivalent thickness of solid brickwork.

The cavity in a cavity-built wall, which is usually about 50 mm (2 in.) wide, can also be filled with an insulating material, provided you make sure the outer surface of the wall is entirely weatherproof. The materials normally used for filling wall cavities are either a kind of plastic foam (injected as a liquid but setting as a solid material full of holes), or mineral wool, which is injected under pressure and remains in the cavities as a mass of fibres. Another method involves filling the cavities with tiny beads of expanded polystyrene.

These methods of insulation have to be carried out by a specialist installer, usually from the outside of the building, and involve drilling a series of holes over the entire surface of the wall from top to bottom. Firms who carry out this work invariably include an estimate for filling the holes afterwards and, in practice, the holes are not very noticeable once the job is complete. This insulation is a

INSULATION

INSULATION

permanent addition to the building and is very cost-effective; you can reckon on the cost of the work being recovered by savings in heating costs within four or five years. Nearly all firms undertaking this kind of work issue a guarantee, although you should also make sure that the firm has an 'Agrément Certificate' relating to its method of installation.

There are a couple of problems associated with the plastic foam method of cavity-wall insulation. First, some people are sensitive to the vapour which is given off when this kind of (UF) plastic, in its liquid form, changes into its honeycomb-type solid form; in extreme cases, this vapour can take years to dissipate. Second, if the installation work is not carried out properly, air pockets may be left inside the cavity; if the outside leaf of the wall is not entirely weathertight, moisture will get into these air pockets where it cannot drain away, and isolated patches of dampness can appear on the inside wall.

It is possible to insulate the outside of external walls and this method is slowly becoming more popular, especially where several houses, close together, can be dealt with at the same time, thus making it an economic proposition. The method involves fixing an insulating material to the outside of the walls and then adding a further weatherproof coating, normally held in place with a concealed wire mesh. It is particularly suitable for solid walls because a thick layer of insulation can be added without reducing the size of the rooms inside. It is a skilled job, requiring special techniques to make sure that window and door openings are modified properly, and that outside rainwater and drainage pipes are moved to take account of the additional wall thickness.

Caution
Before adding an insulation layer to an existing wall, you should make quite sure that the wall is not suffering from rising damp – otherwise dampness will become trapped inside and could cause structural damage.

Similarly, if you are adding an insulation layer to the inside of a solid wall, you should make quite sure that the outside of the wall is completely weatherproof. If you have doubts about dampness in the wall which you want to insulate, get professional advice first. Timber battens, which you fix to the inside of a wall when adding an internal lining, should be pressure-impregnated with preservative; ask a timber merchant about this form of timber treatment. The importance of a vapour barrier has been mentioned above, but cannot be stressed enough; it is essential to make sure that water vapour from within the building cannot get into an enclosed space where it could condense and cause *unseen* damage to the structure.

Windows

Double-glazing will cut down the heat loss through windows by about half, but, as only abut 10 per cent of the total heat loss is through the windows anyway, you can expect to cut down the total heat loss from your house by only about 5 per cent. Professionally-installed double-glazing can be expensive, and the cost involved would take many years to recover in terms of savings on your fuel bills.

Using heavy curtains at the windows can be as good a method as any of reducing heat loss. In times gone by, wooden shutters were used instead of, or in addition to, heavy drapes at the windows. Less extreme measures involve secondary glazing, where a completely independent sheet of glass is fitted, or factory-sealed double-glazed panels, which fit directly into the main window frame or opening casements. For the best heat-saving installation, you should aim for an air space of about 20 mm (¾ in.) between the two pieces of glass; this is usually difficult to achieve in the case of factory-sealed units, which normally have an air space of only about 6–8 mm (¼–⅜ in.).

With these factory-sealed units you have only two sides of glass to keep clean, but with secondary double-glazing there is every chance of dust, or insects, getting in between the two sheets of glass, and you therefore

INSULATION

have twice the area to keep clean. For this reason, secondary double-glazing is best fitted by means of hinged or sliding panels (which also permit ventilation, when required), or with special clips or 'toggles' around the edges of fixed panels so that they can be removed periodically for cleaning.

There are a number of DIY-type double-glazing products on the market, which, despite their inherent drawbacks, are quite cheap and therefore represent good value for money in terms of recovering your initial outlay. These range from semi-permanent methods, involving sheets of perspex which you can fit across the entire window frame, held in place with plastic clips or a special kind of magnetic self-adhesive tape, to a seasonal method whereby you fix a sheet of durable plastic film across the window, held in place with double-sided adhesive tape, and which you make taut by warming it with an electric hairdryer. (The film remains in place for the winter and can then be discarded in warmer weather.)

Caution
You must make sure that you do not double-glaze all of the windows in such a way that you cannot open any of them easily when needed. Cooking smells and steam need to escape from the building, otherwise you run the risk of damage to decorations and clothes from condensation. Do remember that people need oxygen to survive!

If you have a gas multi-point heater or central heating boiler which must draw air from within the room in order to operate properly, you *must* make sure that air can enter the room where the appliance is installed. You must not block up any air bricks or window ventilators which have been provided for supplying combustion air to heating appliances. If you use hair-sprays, or have clothes dry-cleaned, the absence of adequate ventilation could have serious consequences.

Floors
The amount of heat lost through the ground floor is not normally excessive. The simplest method of providing an

insulation layer is by means of a fitted carpet and underlay, or cork tiles. Better insulation can be achieved with a layer of expanded polystyrene panels underneath a wearing surface of chipboard or plywood panels; this method of insulation is commonly adopted in the construction of new buildings nowadays. If you have sufficient space underneath, such as a half-cellar, you could fix expanded polystyrene panels or rigid glass-fibre batts between the floor joists.

Caution
If you have a solid floor surfaced with softwood boards (as was common in houses built around 50 years ago), you must be careful about what you use to cover the floors. Softwood can deteriorate quickly when subjected to moisture over long periods and, if there is any risk of dampness coming up from the solid base underneath, the boarding must be allowed to breathe to allow the moisture to evaporate. To cover such boarding with a vinyl floor covering, or with a rubber carpet underlay, could lead to problems in the future.

Draughts
Stopping draughts, or 'draughtstripping', is the most cost-effective method of keeping the heat in and the cold out. Badly fitting doors and windows allow heat to escape, yet the problem can be overcome quite easily on a DIY basis. Starting at the front door, you can buy a plastic panel which is quite easy to fit over the inside of the letter box, which, by means of fixed nylon brushes, will allow letters to be pushed through, but will keep unwanted draughts out.

Around the edge of the door you can fit one of a whole range of draughtstripping products designed for this purpose, most of which incorporate small-section rubber or plastic piping which pushes up tight to the door when the door is shut. The same product can be used around the inside of opening timber window casements. Only the barest minimum of tools are required to fit this, and no strength or special skill is needed. If you visit your nearest

INSULATION

INSULATION

DIY or hardware shop, you will find a wide range of draught-proofing products and will also be able to obtain advice on which products are best suited to your particular doors and windows.

Certain types of double-glazing will assist in reducing draughts, although the best benefits are to be obtained from using both double-glazing and draughtstripping. Heavy curtains, hung behind external doors throughout the colder months, will also help.

There are now several products on the market which can be used for 'seasonal' draughtstripping. One of these is in the form of a plastic which, like toothpaste, can be squeezed out of a tube to fill the gap between each opening window casement and its frame, and can form an effective method of draughtstripping vertically sliding sash windows. This procedure is only effective, however, if you do not need to open the window. At the end of the winter, you simply peel off and dispose of the plastic strip around each window, which, according to the manufacturers, can be done without damage to the decorations.

Caution
As mentioned above, you should retain some windows which can be opened easily for ventilation when required, and you should *not* block up ventilation openings which are required in connection with heating appliances.

Plumbing
You should make sure that all hot-water pipes and fittings (unless they are designed to heat the rooms in which they are installed) are well insulated. Both hot and cold pipes, and fittings in unheated areas, such as in outbuildings and in roof spaces, should be well insulated to protect them from freezing. Aim to use insulating materials designed for the purpose; try to avoid the use of old blankets, quilts and newspaper, which can attract moths and vermin, and, in any case, could be a fire risk.

Water pipes are best insulated during installation, with tubular sleeves which are slipped on over the pipes before they are connected together. Pipework already in place can be insulated with a kind of hessian wrapping (put on like a bandage), or with tubular sleeves of foam or aerated rubber which are split down one side, pushed over the pipes, and then held in place with adhesive tape. Sectional pipe insulation, made of mineral wool in a rigid form, is held in place over the pipes with metal clips. Whichever of these products is used, the adjoining lengths should be trimmed with a sharp knife to fit around bends and fittings.

The hot-water storage cylinder has a large surface area from which heat can be lost, and yet this is probably the easiest part of your home to insulate. You simply have to measure the height and diameter of the cylinder and purchase a sectional insulating jacket which is held in position with draw-strings. The jacket should have a thickness of 80–100 mm and should not be squashed flat (as the lightweight nature of its glass-fibre filling is what provides the insulation, like a duvet). If the cylinder is fitted with a thermostat or an electric immersion heater, then these and their connecting cables should be exposed and not concealed underneath the insulation jacket.

Cold-water storage cisterns in roof spaces should always be well insulated. They should also be provided with close-fitting rigid covers (which, in any case, is normally a requirement of the local water authority). It was at one time fashionable to build an enclosure around the cold-water cistern, leaving a space of about 100 mm (4 in.), which was then filled with an insulating material such as wood shavings. This method had inherent disadvantages and, with the advent of new building materials, alternative methods have been adopted. Panels, or slabs, of expanded polystyrene can be held in position around the cistern or, perhaps better still, a glass-fibre-filled insulating jacket can be purchased for the particular size of the cistern and this, like that around the hot-water storage cylinder, is held in place with draw-strings. The underside of the cistern should not be insulated, to

INSULATION

INSULATION

enable a small amount of heat to rise from the rooms below and reach the cistern itself to prevent the water from freezing.

Caution

In older properties, you may find pipework, especially in the roof space, which has been insulated with a thick coating of a white or brown fibrous substance. Although this might constitute a satisfactory form of insulation, it can, in some cases, contain asbestos fibres, which could be harmful if inhaled.

If you discover this kind of material in your home, you should not disturb it, but, instead, seek professional advice. The usual procedure is for a small sample to be removed, with the minimum of disturbance, and sent for laboratory analysis. If asbestos fibres are found to be present, the insulation should be sealed up and left in place, or removed from the property by a licensed asbestos removal firm, depending on the type of asbestos and other factors. You should *not* attempt to remove or dispose of asbestos insulation yourself.

Value for money

The installation cost of some methods of insulation is soon recovered in fuel-bill savings: the cost of draught-stripping, for example, could be recovered in about three to four weeks; the cost of a proper jacket for your hot-water storage could be recovered in about a month – if you heat your water by full-price electricity. (These estimates assume that you would undertake these jobs yourself.)

A priority list for insulation measures, expressed in terms of value for money, is as follows:

Draught proofing
Hot-water cylinder jacket
Loft insulation
Wall insulation
Double-glazing

Grants

You might be able to get a grant from your local authority towards the cost of insulating your home. At the time of going to press, the ruling was that you had to be in receipt of supplementary benefit, or a rent or rate rebate, that the property must have been built before 1975, and that there must be a thickness of not more than 30 mm (1 in.) insulation in the roof space before a grant would be considered. If these conditions apply to you, you could be entitled to a grant of up to 90 per cent of the cost of insulating your home. For further advice, ask at your local authority offices (where you pay your rates).

Electricity

Electricity is dangerous. You must always keep that in mind, and make sure you protect yourself from that danger. Remember that more than 1000 fires are caused each year by electrical faults, and around 40 people are killed each year by faulty wiring in England and Wales alone. Although it is out of sight, and all too often out of mind, you should make sure your electrical installation is all that you expect it to be.

Get to know your electricity supply

The Electricity Board's cable enters your house and terminates in a bulky fuse, with two thick cables to the meter. These cables and equipment are the property of the Electricity Board and you have no right to tamper with them. There may be two or more meters, and a timeclock if you have an off-peak supply as well as a standard supply.

Another pair of cables then runs from the meter to your own fuseboard, and these and the rest of the installation belong to you.

If you live in a flat, the Electricity Board's fuse and meter might be in a special cupboard, together with

ELECTRICITY

those of the other flats; this way, it is easier for the Board to read several meters at the same time. Even in single houses it is becoming commonplace for the meter to be located in an outside box (so that you are not disturbed when meter readings have to be taken), with the fuseboard inside. If the main supply is underground, as is commonly the case, the Board will almost certainly provide an 'earth' cable in addition to the 'live' and 'neutral' cables, and the earth circuits of your own installation may be connected to this. Looking at the insulation covering of these main cables, live is red, neutral is black, and earth is green, whereas, for modern domestic flex insulation, live is brown, neutral is blue, and earth is either green, or yellow and green striped.

There are still many parts of the country where the main electricity supply cables are carried overhead, between poles, and not run underground. If you live in one of these areas the cables will almost certainly connect to your house at insulated terminals outdoors, fixed at high level. They will then be run to the Board's fuse and meter indoors. In many rural areas, the Electricity Board does not provide an earth, and it is your responsibility to do this by means of a green insulated cable connected to a metal rod driven into the ground. In cases such as this, there should be an RCD (residual current device) or RCCB (residual current circuit breaker) to the earth connection. This device is a form of main switch which automatically switches off the supply if an 'earthing' fault develops in the installation.

Your fuseboard

The design of your fuseboard will depend to some extent on when your house was built, and on the system adopted at that time for the power circuits.

Wooden fuse boxes are now uncommon (fortunately!) and those still in existence are probably at least 50 years old. Metal boxes, each holding one or two ceramic fuses, with separate boxes for lighting and power circuits, are likely to be at least 40 years old. Single consumer units, made of metal or hard plastic, holding a row of plug-in, rewireable fuses, and with a single main switch, were first used around 30 years ago (*see Figure 22*).

Old-fashioned arrangement

Figure 22

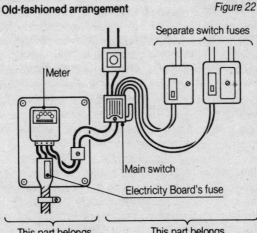

Separate switch fuses

Meter

Main switch

Electricity Board's fuse

This part belongs to the Electricity Board

This part belongs to you

Modern arrangement

Figure 23

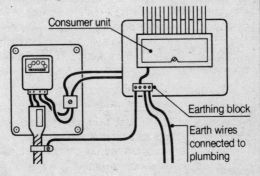

Consumer unit

Earthing block

Earth wires connected to plumbing

In the past 15 years or so, consumer units have tended

ELECTRICITY

to be of the type incorporating miniature circuit-breakers. Miniature circuit-breakers look like ordinary switches but operate like fuses; instead of a fuse blowing, the circuit-breaker switch automatically switches itself off, and can be switched on again only when the fault has been put right. MCBs, as they are usually called, are fully enclosed and are therefore not subject to misuse in the same way as rewireable fuses. Modern consumer units always contain a main switch, often of the RCCB type which turns itself off in the event of a major short circuit, and can also incorporate timeclocks and bell transformers in the same enclosure (*see Figure 23, page 123*).

Consumer unit with rewireable fuses   *Figure 24*

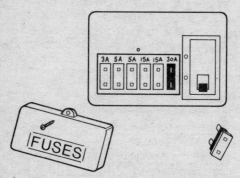

Consumer unit with miniature circuit breakers

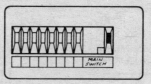

Power circuits

Power outlets are connected to the fuseboard either by radial circuits or ring circuits (*see Figure 25, page 126*). Prior to about 40 years ago all connections were by means of radial circuits, where each socket outlet was connected to an individual fuse at the fuseboard; in other words, all of the circuits radiated from the fuseboard. Over the past 40 years, however, socket outlets have been connected on a ring circuit and it is the ring of socket outlets which has a single fuse, or circuit-breaker, at the fuseboard, not every socket outlet. Because there is a limit to the maximum current which a ring circuit can take, larger houses have two or more separate ring circuits, often arranged with one ring circuit per floor level.

It is still usual practice for radial connections to be provided for electric cookers and immersion heaters, each with their own fuse or circuit-breaker, because they have a heavy electrical demand.

If you have your house rewired you might find it convenient also to have separate radial circuits to the central heating control panel and to the socket outlet for the deep freeze; if you then leave the house unoccupied for any length of time, you would have the option of turning off all the power circuits except just those two.

Enough power points?
A report, issued as long ago as 1975 by the Electrical Installation Liaison Committee, recommended the minimum number of socket outlets in domestic buildings to be as follows (each of these to be a twin, switched type):

Kitchen	4
Living-room	6
Dining-room	3
Double bedroom	4
Single bedroom	3
Single bed-sitting room	4
Landing/stairs	1
Hall	1
Garage	2

If your home was not provided with this number of power outlets, do not simply extend the original circuits without first checking whether the cables can take the extra load

ELECTRICITY

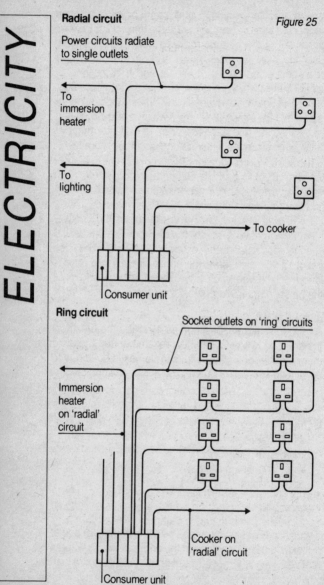

Radial circuit

Figure 25

Power circuits radiate to single outlets

To immersion heater

To lighting

To cooker

Consumer unit

Ring circuit

Socket outlets on 'ring' circuits

Immersion heater on 'radial' circuit

Cooker on 'radial' circuit

Consumer unit

(see below). It could be that your house has only one ring circuit – where two (or even three) ring circuits should now be provided to cater for the number of socket outlets and appliances you want to use.

How old is your electrical installation?
The types of cables and fittings in use have changed over the years and you might gain a clue to the age of the installation in your own home simply from their outward appearance.

Before 1920, cables were insulated with a rubber sleeving, having an outer covering of cotton braid, and were normally enclosed in wooden trunking. Light switches were circular in shape, made of brass, and fixed to wooden mounting blocks; ceiling roses were large china fittings. Socket outlets had two circular holes, and the main fuses were usually housed in wooden boxes.

Up to 1939, rubber-insulated cables sometimes had a lead outer covering. These cables were fixed to the surface of the walls and joinery, and connected at junction boxes made of thin-gauge steel.

A different kind of cable, in use between 1925 and 1935, had a tough rubber outer casing with a flat section in between the two wires; the cable was fixed in position with nails driven through the flat section of rubber. Earth wires were rarely provided to socket outlets before 1935.

Rubber-insulated cables continued in use up to about 1960, often being enclosed in metal conduits (tubes) fixed to the surfaces of walls and ceilings. The later versions of this type of cable had a tough rubber outer covering, and socket outlets used at that time usually had circular holes.

Cables in which the wires are insulated with a PVC sleeving, and which have a flat PVC outer covering, usually grey or white in colour, have been in use since 1950.

Socket outlets introduced at that time were of the 13-amp, square-hole type, although early versions were not fitted with integral switches. Earth wires on lighting cables were not obligatory until 1967.

ELECTRICITY

ELECTRICITY

A quite different kind of cable, sometimes found these days in domestic buildings, perhaps where associated with external wiring, is mineral-insulated copper-covered (MICC) cable. It is expensive, and is normally used only in commercial buildings.

Different sizes of cable
Modern PVC-insulated cables of the type you are most likely to find in your home are manufactured in a range of sizes to suit different electrical loads – the wires themselves (the conductors) inside the cables are of specific sizes to cater for the electrical loads they have to carry.

Most of the cables used for lighting circuits, for example, contain conductors which have a cross-sectional area of 1 sq mm, whereas cables designed for power circuits contain conductors which have a cross-sectional area of 2.5 sq mm. Cables used for cooker circuits contain conductors which are bigger still. The early types of PVC-insulated cables had conductors which consisted of several strands of wire – with the total cross-sectional area of the strands being equivalent to the single-wire conductor found in modern cables used for lighting and power circuits.

Whereas in PVC-covered cables the two main (live and neutral) wires have a PVC sleeving, the earth wire does not have its own insulation. Where exposed, however, as inside light switches and socket outlets, the earth wire should always be fitted separately with a yellow and green striped PVC sleeving.

Flush-mounted light switches and socket outlets should be fitted to recessed metal boxes, and the earth wire in the cable should always be securely clamped to the earthing screw in the metal box.

It is important to ensure that cables do not become overloaded. Socket outlets should never be connected to lighting circuits, for example, and power circuits should not be extended by the addition of more socket outlets, or with lots of multi-outlet adaptors, unless a qualified electrician has checked the capacity of the circuits.

Some protection against overloading will be afforded by the main fuses, or circuit-breakers, but it is important not to fit larger-capacity fuses than those installed, or the cables themselves could overheat and cause a fire.

Protecting cables
Although PVC-covered cables are quite durable, they should be protected from physical damage where exposed within rooms or where concealed in walls just behind the plaster.

You can get rectangular-shaped plastic trunking, of small cross section (to hold just two or three cables), or in larger sizes, to use instead of skirtings along the bottom of walls, for example, and in either case there is an accompanying range of interlocking connection pieces to make sure the cables inside are fully protected. If you have any loose cables around your home, they can be concealed using this method; you would need to ask an electrical contractor or wholesaler for further details of the sizes and connection pieces available.

Plastic tubing, either circular or oval in cross section, is normally used to protect cables which are to be concealed by plaster or wallboarding; specially shaped sections of thin-gauge steel are also used for this purpose.

When houses are built, it is common practice for this tubing to be fixed to the surface of a brick or blockwork wall and then plastered over, so there may be only about 6 mm (¼ in.) of plaster covering the cables. If you are a keen do-it-yourselfer, you should buy a small electronic gadget now on the market, which, by means of a flashing light and buzzer, locates concealed pipes and cables. This can be purchased for just a few pounds – a small price to pay for peace of mind when drilling holes in walls.

PVC-covered cables should be protected from coming into contact with expanded polystyrene insulation, in roof spaces, for example, because a chemical interaction between the two materials affects the plastic around the cables and makes it sticky.

ELECTRICITY

ELECTRICITY

For safety's sake

Make a few checks to see how safe you are at home:

- The light switch in your bathroom should be of the pull-cord type; conventional wall switches or lamps should never be positioned where they can be touched by anyone with wet hands.

- Shaver sockets in bathrooms should be of a special kind designed for that purpose; ordinary two-pin socket outlets will not do. You should never have any other kind of socket outlet in a bathroom – and you should not use portable electric appliances in bathrooms – even if they are on a long flex, plugged in elsewhere.

- Plumbing below sinks, baths, basins, etc., should be fitted with a special clip around each of the pipes and wired to a common earth terminal near the fuseboard. This cross-bonding, as it is called, is a requirement of modern safety regulations and has become necessary in view of the increasing number of plastic pipes and fittings used for plumbing, which can no longer be relied upon for satisfactory earthing.

- Avoid the use of multi-outlet adaptors throughout the house as much as you can. They could overload the power circuits. If you do not have enough socket outlets, ask a qualified electrician to check whether any more can be wired off the existing power circuits (in the form of spurs), or whether additional circuits are necessary to avoid overloading.

- Are the socket outlets too low? They are sometimes installed so close to the floor that, when you plug in, the flex is bent very sharply and can become damaged. Socket outlets at table-top level make sense for appliances such as electric irons, hairdriers, etc., and an added benefit here is that you do not have to stoop to use them. Think about this if you have additional sockets installed.

● An appliance such as a washing machine, sited near a sink, is best wired to a special connection unit. This does the same job as a socket outlet, except that there is no plug or socket – the appliance flex is wired directly to the unit. Connection units of this kind have a cartridge fuse located inside them; some have a switch fitted, usually of a double-pole type, where, instead of just the live conductor being switched, the neutral conductor is also switched at the same time.

● If you use electrical equipment out of doors (an electric mower, drill, etc.), always plug in to a socket which incorporates a residual current circuit-breaker (RCB), sometimes also called a residual current device (RCD). This kind of socket incorporates a special switch which turns itself off automatically in the event of an earth fault. You can now buy portable RCD sockets which you plug into ordinary sockets; they are not expensive.

● An advisory leaflet, published some years ago by the Department of the Environment, recommends that you have your electrical installation checked every five years to see whether it complies with the latest IEE Regulations (published by the Institution of Electrical Engineers). If you have not had a check carried out for some time, then get this done by a properly qualified electrician.

● The *golden rule* is – never play about with your house wiring unless you really know what you are doing. And if you employ someone else, make sure *they* know what they are doing. Anyone can set up in business as an electrician, without having any proper qualifications, so be careful whom you employ. The ECA (Electrical Contractors Association) runs a scheme which guarantees the work of its members. The NICEIC (National Inspection Council for Electrical Installation Contracting) keeps a list of approved electrical contractors and checks their standard of work

ELECTRICITY

ELECTRICITY

periodically; you can see a copy of the list at public libraries and Electricity Board showrooms.

Plugging in

Frayed or damaged flex, or flex that looks very old, should be renewed. Unless you feel confident about reconnecting new flex to an appliance yourself, get it done at a reputable shop which carries out repairs to household electrical appliances. Flexible cable is manufactured in a range of thicknesses, so, if you do the job yourself, be sure to use a flex of the appropriate rating for the appliance (see page 133).

The same applies if the flex on the appliance is not long enough. Do not try to join two lengths of wire together with tape around them; either fit a new, longer length of flex, or use an extension lead supplied with cable of the appropriate rating for the appliance.

Fit a plug on the flex yourself only if you feel confident about this. Remember, the brown (or red) wire in the flex should be connected to the terminal marked 'Live' or 'L'; the blue (or black) wire should be connected to the terminal marked 'Neutral' or 'N'; the green and yellow striped (or green) wire is connected to the terminal marked 'Earth' or 'E'. Always use the two cable-grip screws, with the clamping strip between them, to hold the flex firmly in place, but do not overtighten these screws. Some modern plugs have a pair of fixed plastic clips, instead of cable-grip screws, to secure the flex in place. The 13-amp plug tops now manufactured have to have protected (insulated) pins, so make sure you are not sold one of the old types which do not have this safety feature.

The principal advantage which modern square-pin plugs have over the old-fashioned round-pin types is that they are designed to contain a fuse. The reason for this is that a fault in the appliance or flex will cause the plug fuse to blow, without necessarily affecting the whole circuit. But although they are known as 13-amp plugs, and although they are usually sold complete with a 13-amp fuse cartridge inside, this does not mean they should automatically be used with a fuse of this capacity. You can also buy 3- and 5-amp fuse cartridges for use with lower-powered appliances and you should fit the correct fuse cartridge into the plug to suit the appliance.

The current rating (in amps) is sometimes shown on a small metal plate fixed to an appliance, but more often the appliance is marked with its power consumption in watts or kilowatts. (One kilowatt is 1000 watts.)

If you know the power consumption, you can use simple arithmetic to calculate the current which the appliance requires. The standard formula is:

Current (in amps) = power consumption (watts), divided by the voltage (usually 240 volts).

Example 1
For a radio with a power rating of 80 watts: $\frac{80}{240}$ =0.33. In other words, the current used is 0.33 amps, i.e., less than 3 amps, so use a 3-amp fuse cartridge in the plug.

Example 2
For an electric fire with a rating of 3 kilowatts: $\frac{3000}{240}$ =12.5. The maximum current used is 12.5 amps, i.e., more than 3 amps but less than 13 amps, so use a 13-amp fuse cartridge in the plug.

The same calculation is used to determine the current rating of the flex to be used with the appliance.

Problems with electrical installations
There are five main reasons why your electrical installation might be hazardous:

1 Old age
If your wiring has rubber insulation, the chances are that the rubber will have perished or become brittle with age. This usually happens where the wiring gets hot, such as above light fittings and adjoining electric immersion heaters, but it can occur elsewhere. If brittle sections of rubber insulation break away, the wires themselves can touch each other, causing a short circuit, or fire.

ELECTRICITY

ELECTRICITY

2 Outdated design

You can see for yourself whether the bathroom light switch is on the wall or whether a pull-cord switch is installed, and you can also see whether the socket outlets are the round-pin or square-pin type. But you may not be able to tell as easily whether there is an earth wire on the lighting circuits, or whether there are adequate 'cross bonding' earth wires connected to the plumbing. Ineffective earthing means that a short circuit could give you an electric shock.

3 Cables and fittings under-rated

Today we all use many more electrical appliances than people did several years ago. It is quite possible that the power circuits in your home were never intended to supply the number of socket outlets or appliances now in use. Fuses might blow, but there is also a danger that socket outlets and the cables themselves could heat up if you overload the circuits. Never fit a fuse at the main fusebox which is larger than the capacity it is supposed to be. If a fuse keeps blowing, it is because there is a fault in the circuit and it is this which needs attention, *not* the fuse.

The maximum ratings of fuses or miniature circuit-breakers at the main fusebox should be as follows:

Lighting circuits	5 amps
Radial power circuits (e.g., immersion heater)	15 or 20 amps
Ring power circuits	30 amps
Electric cooker	30 or 45 amps depending on the cable size and length

4 Physical damage

Cables which run directly under floorboards can get squashed, and cables in walls with inadequate protection can become damaged. Accidental damage can occur when building repairs and alterations are carried out. If the insulation sleeving is damaged, the wires themselves can touch each other, causing a short circuit or fire.

5 Incorrect installation

This is often the result of electrical work having been carried out by someone other than a properly qualified electrician. Power circuits can become overloaded by the addition of too many socket outlets; earth wires might not be connected, and the live and neutral wires could be wrongly connected (a situation known as reversed polarity) which, for example, can mean that cables to a light fitting are live even when the switch is switched off.

Just because 13-amp socket outlets, or modern light switches, are fitted, it does not mean that the installation has necessarily been rewired. Old rubber-insulated cables could have been retained and reconnected to new surface fittings. In cases such as this, the old cables can sometimes be seen in the loft, or at the main fuseboard.

Flood damage

If you have a burst pipe or a serious roof leak, which lets water get into parts of the electrical installation, you run the risk of short circuits and possible corrosion in the fittings. In the event of such an occurrence, you should have the electrical installation tested immediately, and then once a month for a period of six months, by which time any moisture should have dried out.

WHAT TO LOOK OUT FOR

ELECTRICAL PROBLEMS

▶ **Symptom**

a No power from a socket outlet or connection unit.

b A fuse in the main fuseboard keeps blowing.

c There are scorch marks around the holes of a socket outlet. A socket outlet or plug top gets hot.

d The flex to a plug gets hot.

ELECTRICITY

ELECTRICITY

e Sparks fly from a light switch or from the switch on a socket outlet when the switch is operated.
f The plastic surround to a ceiling rose, or a lamp surround, is cracked or broken.

▶ **Cause**

a A fuse has blown in the plug top or connection unit.
b (i) The fuse used is rated too low for the circuit.
　(ii) The circuit is overloaded.
　(iii) There is a fault in the circuit.
c (i) There are loose wires to the terminal screws.
　(ii) A faulty plug or socket.
　(iii) The socket is drawing too much current (this can happen if an electric motor, e.g. in a washing machine, is overloaded).
d The flex is of insufficient rating, or the flex is coiled.
e A faulty switch.
f There is excessive heat from the lamp.

▶ **Remedy**

a (i) Check and replace the fuse in the plug top or connection unit.
　(ii) Check and replace the fuse in the main fuseboard.
b (i) Replace the fuse with a fuse of the correct capacity – *not* a fuse with a higher capacity filament.
　(ii) Switch off or unplug all appliances from the power circuit. Replace all fuses with those of the correct capacity. Plug in and switch on appliances at each socket in turn.
　(iii) Consult a qualified electrician.
c (i) Check the screw terminals inside the plug top. Check the cartridge fuse for the correct rating for the appliance.
　(ii) Renew the plug top, or get an electrician to renew the socket outlet plate.

   (iii) Do not overload appliances which contain
      electric motors.
d Have the flex rating checked by taking the
appliance to an electrical repairer. Have a new flex
fitted if necessary. Make sure the flex is never coiled;
coiled flex to high-rated appliances acts like a
heating element and can get extremely hot.
e Renew the switch or socket outlet plate.
f Renew the fitting. Consider using a lower-wattage
bulb.

Gas

Mains gas is a convenient form of fuel available in most
parts of the UK, except in rural areas. If you want to use
mains gas, but do not already have a piped supply to your
home, ask your nearest British Gas office whether there
is a gas main nearby from which they could make a connection available to you. If the nearest gas main is some
distance away, and an individual connection would not
be an economic proposition, British Gas might be persuaded to extend the main if several houses, close
together, all want a gas supply. You would need to get
together with your neighbours to explore this possibility.

Get to know your gas supply
An individual service pipe runs into your property and terminates at a stop valve to which a gas meter is connected. The gas meter has to be located in a position
which is well ventilated and where it cannot get damp.
These days an increasing number of meters are housed
in glass-fibre boxes, fitted externally. This enables the
meter to be read periodically without you having to be at
home to let the meter reader come inside the house.
Meters already fitted indoors can be repositioned externally in a box in this manner, but you would have to pay
British Gas for making the alteration. The stop valve and

GAS

meter belong to British Gas and must not be tampered with by you.

You are, however, allowed to turn off the gas supply at the stop valve in an emergency. The stop valve is invariably operated by a lever, which usually has a small line engraved on it over the top of the valve. The valve is in the on position when the lever (and the engraved line) are pointing in the same direction as the pipe; and in the off position when they are pointing at right angles to the pipe.

Your gas installation
All gas pipework and fittings in your home must comply with the Gas Safety Regulations, which exist for your protection. Although natural gas itself is not poisonous, leaking pipework or inadequate ventilation could have serious consequences.

Where gas pipes are boxed in, the space (or duct) enclosing the pipe should be ventilated to the outside air, and the area (e.g., cupboard) where the gas meter is installed should be ventilated in a similar manner. This is to avoid the risk of explosion which could result from an accumulation of gas in an enclosed space.

Unless you know you are fully competent to work on your gas installation, you should entrust this task to a British Gas engineer, or to a CORGI (Confederation of Registered Gas Installers) registered firm.

Except in the case of small appliances with low gas consumption, such as gas cookers and small gas water-heaters, which are designed to operate without a flue, gas appliances must have effective flues which discharge direct to the outside air – not into the roof space.

A gas-burning appliance which has a conventional flue (to a chimney) must have a permanent supply of air to it for combustion; you must be careful about this when draughtstripping or when having double-glazing installed, and you should never block up air bricks or window ventilators which have been fitted for the purpose of supplying combustion air to the gas appliance.

Problems with gas installations

Problems tend to be either gas leaks (gas escapes) or the malfunction of gas-burning appliances. Normally these can be detected by the smell of gas.

Whereas underground gas pipes were at one time made of iron, and were susceptible to corrosion and consequent gas leaks, British Gas have, in recent years, had a programme of replacing underground pipes with modern plastic materials which do not corrode. If the incoming gas service pipe to the stop valve next to your meter is made of plastic (usually a yellow colour) you are less likely to be troubled by problems in the underground section of pipework than if it is made of iron.

If you detect a smell of gas in your home, the first thing to do is to turn off all gas appliances, turn off the main supply (at the stop valve) and open all windows and doors to disperse any accumulation of gas. Naked lights should be put out, of course, and cigarettes should be extinguished immediately by immersing them in water. If the smell of gas disappears after the main valve has been turned off, the problem is in the pipework inside your house. Sometimes, it can be traced to an unlit pilot light or to a gas cooker, for example, where one of the burners has blown out. If you are in any doubt about the cause of a gas leak, contact British Gas immediately (the telephone number is in your telephone directory under Gas), or get a competent gas engineer to locate and repair the fault.

You will be less likely to suffer problems from malfunction if you have all gas appliances serviced on a regular basis. You can then expect gas valves, pilot lights and burners to be kept in good condition. Servicing contracts can be taken out with British Gas or with a CORGI-registered installer.

GAS

Insurance

INSURANCE

Claiming on your insurance

If you suffer a catastrophe you might be covered by insurance for the cost of putting right any damage to your building. If a claim is ultimately going to be accepted by your insurers, however, there are two things you must do straight away.

1 You must 'mitigate your loss' – in other words, take whatever action is necessary to prevent the damage getting any worse.

2 Notify your insurers immediately.

Mitigating your loss

If you have a fire, for example, and part of the roof is destroyed, you should arrange for a tarpaulin to be securely fixed over the roof to keep the structure weathertight. This is often done by the fire brigade on a temporary basis, but you may need to employ a local builder to carry out a more secure job until permanent reconstruction can be undertaken. Sometimes this is not possible for many weeks.

In the event of a burst pipe or a plumbing leak, for example, you must turn off the water at the mains, and you should not use any pipework that is likely to cause further leaks. Where stopcocks are found to be jammed, and cannot be turned off, it may even be necessary to hammer the pipe flat to stop the flow of water.

Notifying your insurers

If you pay your building insurance premium direct to an insurance company, then contact that company yourself. If, as is more likely, your home insurance is undertaken by your building society or bank, then contact the relevant branch office and tell them you want to make a claim on your policy. In either case, ask the organisation to send you a claim form.

You might find that what you receive is a multi-purpose form dealing with burglary and so on, and in this case there will be certain sections which are not applicable to physical damage to the building. It is unlikely at this stage that you will have had time to obtain estimates for repair costs. Do not make guesses at these, but mark the form 'estimates not yet obtained'. The claim form must be completed and returned as soon as possible, so that your insurers are notified with the minimum of delay.

If you do not already have a specimen policy, with all its small print, then now is the time to ask for a copy. Do not rely on the 'Summary of Cover' leaflet if you want to find out exactly what is covered and what is not. For claims under certain sections of the policy, you are likely to find that you will be reimbursed for the cost of surveyors' fees incurred by you in connection with reconstruction work.

What happens next

In the case of a substantial claim, your insurers will almost certainly employ an independent firm of loss adjusters to investigate your claim on their behalf. A representative, or surveyor, from that firm will contact you and all further discussions will be with that individual. Most loss adjusters have many years' experience of dealing with the kind of problem which you now have to face. You will normally find them helpful and they will guide you on what to do next. The loss adjuster will not be as co-operative, however, if you try to press a claim for more than that to which you are entitled.

You could find it much less of a burden to engage a professional surveyor to act on your behalf, and to undertake all negotiations with the loss adjuster. You can obtain the names of suitable surveyors in your area by contacting the information centre at the Royal Institution of Chartered Surveyors (RICS) - telephone 01-222 7000 (in Scotland, 031-225 7078). Find out what the surveyor would charge, and ask the loss adjuster whether all, or any, of the surveyor's fees will be admissible as part of your claim. Most policies do not cover you for professional fees incurred in negotiating the claim itself, but only for fees directly related to the task of reconstruction.

If the damage is so extensive that you have to move out

INSURANCE

of your house, either before or during the reconstruction work, your policy may cover you for the cost of alternative accommodation. Many policies have a maximum limit on such costs, however, and you should check this with the policy document, and with the loss adjuster.

The question of 'average'
One of the first things the loss adjuster is likely to do when he first calls is to assess whether your property is insured for its full value. If he feels the building is significantly under-insured he will no doubt tell you so, and he may say that your claim could be subject to 'average'. This means that you might only be reimbursed in the same proportion to the amount for which you have insured the house (compared with its full value). For example, if the full cost of reconstructing your house is £80,000 and you have it insured for only £60,000, it would be regarded as insured for only 75 per cent of its full value. Your insurers might then apply average and pay you only 75 per cent of the value of your claim.

You must, therefore, make sure your house is insured for the full cost of total reconstruction. This is not the price that it would fetch if sold. The cost of reconstruction is usually less than this, but can sometimes be more.

Getting paid
If your insurance company accepts a claim (based on the recommendations of their appointed loss adjuster), you are likely to be reimbursed after you have had the reinstatement work carried out, i.e., when the actual cost of reinstatement is known. Where the claim is for a substantial sum of money, your insurers might be prepared to make payments 'on account'. In exceptional circumstances, your insurers might be prepared to pay your builder direct, but you would have to ask them first.

When the repair works have been completed, set out a summary of your total claim. This might include:

● temporary (emergency) works, such as keeping the building weathertight;

- the cost of building work (based on the builder's final account); local authority fees, if you have had to pay these under the Building Regulations;
- the amount charged by the Electricity Board or British Gas, if their services have been affected;
- professional fees, if you have employed a surveyor;
- the cost of temporary accommodation (if this was agreed at the outset).

When everything has been put right, and when you have notified the loss adjuster of all your costs, you will no doubt be sent a form to sign to confirm that the total figure is the full amount which you are accepting in settlement of the claim. It is unlikely that you will receive the full amount from your insurers until that form has been signed and returned. It is important, therefore, to ensure that no costs have been omitted, as your insurers are unlikely to entertain a claim for further expenses afterwards.

Don't panic!

Fire
IMMEDIATELY
Get everyone out of the building.
Telephone 999 and ask for 'Fire'.
Warn your neighbours.
Turn off gas and electricity at the mains (see pages 124 and 138).
WHEN THE FIRE IS OUT
Get a builder to make sure your house is structurally safe and weathertight.
If it is insecure, tell the police.
If the structure is damaged, tell your insurers (see page 140).

Smell of gas
Turn off gas at the mains (see page 138).
Telephone British Gas (look under GAS in your phone book) or call in a reliable plumber.

DON'T PANIC!

Electrical problems
Turn off electricity at the mains (see page 124).
Telephone your Electricity Board (look under
ELECTRICITY in your phone book) or call in a
registered electrician (see page 131).

Struck by lightning
If there is any sign of fire, see FIRE above.
Turn off electricity at the mains (see page 124).
Telephone your Electricity Board (look under
ELECTRICITY in your phone book), or call in a
registered electrician (see page 131); lightning can
seriously damage electrical installations.
Get a builder to make sure your house is structurally
safe and weathertight.
If it is insecure, tell the police. If the structure
is damaged, tell your insurers (see page 140).

Burst pipe
Turn off water at the main stopcock (see page 81).
Telephone your Water Authority (look under WATER
in your phone book) or call in a reliable plumber.
If you think water might have got into any parts of the
electrical installation, telephone your Electricity Board
(look under ELECTRICITY in your phone book) or call
in a registered electrician (see pages 131 and 135).
If the structure is damaged, tell your insurers (see
page 140).

Blocked drain
Locate and clear the blockage (see page 44).
If the drain has broken, tell your insurers (see page
140).

Cracks in the building
Get a building surveyor to tell you whether there is
any immediate danger; and ask the surveyor for a
report. (See pages 24 and 66.)
Tell your insurers (see page 140).